Father
Fell Down
the Well

By Kendall Morse

Other humor books from Islandport Press

Huntin' and Fishin' with the Ole Man
Dave O'Connor

Finding Your Inner Moose
Susan Poulin

Bert and I . . . The Book
Marshall Dodge and Robert Bryan

A Moose and a Lobster Walk into a Bar
John McDonald

Live Free and Eat Pie!
Rebecca Rule

Welcome to Frost Heaves
Fred Marple

See all of our books at
www.islandportpress.com

Father
Fell Down
the Well

Classic Stories from Downeast

By Kendall Morse

ISLANDPORT PRESS

Islandport Press
P.O. Box 10
Yarmouth, Maine 04096
www.islandportpress.com

ISBN: 978-1-939017-21-5
Library of Congress Control Number: 2015946882

First Islandport edition published August 2015

Dean L. Lunt, Publisher
Book cover design by Karen F. Hoots / Hoots Design
Book design by Michelle A. Lunt / Islandport Press
Author cover image by Dean L. Lunt
Author back cover and page 113 image by Kevin Bennett

Usually it is nearly impossible to trace a story back to its origins; however, one of the exceptions I have found is a story titled *Father Fell Down the Well.*
This story was created by the late Steve Merrill.
This book is dedicated to the memory of that outstanding humorist and writer.
Thanks Steve.

-KM

Contents

Foreword

The state of Maine is unique in many ways, but I'd like to explore just one of them in this book: Humor.

With the exceptions of Vermont and Texas, Maine stands alone in its rich tradition of regional humor. No one seems able to explain how this came about, so my guess is as good as yours, so to speak.

Maybe it's the climate: ten months of winter, followed by Mud Season, and then thirty days of fog. Or maybe it's the economic situation here: We seem to have the highest taxes and lowest employment of any state.

If you live in Maine, you have three choices for dealing with the weather and the economy:

1) Be born rich or become rich.

2) Get out. Most Mainers won't even consider this; if you can't take the winters, you don't deserve the summers, is their view.

3) Find the humor in it all.

Kendall Morse   ix

Number three is my favorite, and if enough people buy this book, I will be able to explore choice number one.

Thanks for reading,
Kendall Morse
August 2015

Chapter 1

Grover Pays a Visit

I live about two miles up the Ebb Tide Road in a house that was built by my grandfather. It's well over a hundred years old, and will probably be around for another hundred. Houses don't have many natural enemies in our small town on the Maine coast. It is a great little town in many ways—full of characters and full of stories. You can choose to believe them if you want, but you do so at your own risk.

Me and the missus and our three girls live here in the old homestead year-round, if you can call it living. The summer is real nice, what with the sea breeze and all, but the winter gets quite savage. Someone once told me that Maine was God's Country. I replied, "That might be, but he don't spend the winter's here."

There are four rooms downstairs and three up, but in the winter we close off one of the downstairs rooms to save on heat, so we spend a lot of time in the kitchen. The parlor is reserved for important company, such as the preacher and the ladies' sewing circle.

The old kitchen is pretty much as it was when Mother was alive, although we did swap the old hand pump on the sink for an electric pump in the cellar, and the old icebox went to the dump years ago, having been replaced by a refrigerator. For entertainment, we rely pretty much on ourselves, and one of the things we enjoy most is having someone drop in for an evening of checkers, or just yarning.

One day last winter it was colder than a dead man's tongue, and I was sitting around trying to keep my pipe going when I heard someone stamping the snow off his feet on the front steps. The piazza is on the front of the house, facing south. In the summer it's a nice place to sit and watch the boats coming and going out in the harbor, and, in the winter, having the front door face south helps keep the heat in when someone goes in or out. Around here the north wind is called the Montreal Express, and if the door was on the north side, it would blow the dishes off the table and quick-freeze whatever was on them.

I wasn't expecting anyone, so when I opened the door I was both surprised and pleased to see Grover Furlong standing there with an icicle hanging off the tip of his long nose.

"Godfrey mighty, Grover!" I said. "What are you doing out on a rafter snapper night like this?"

"Didn't realize how cold it was," he said. "I broke my glasses and can't see the thermometer. That mercury is getting shorter and harder to read every day now. Besides, the old woman was getting on my nerves, jawing about one thing and another all the time."

"That woman's got more mouth than a government mule," I said.

"Ayuh, of course, I don't help much," he said. "This morning I called her 'Angel,' and when she asked why, I told her that it was because she was always up in the air, harping about something. She hasn't run down yet."

"Come in, Grover," I said. "I was just about to put the kettle on."

Now, making a pot of tea is not a casual undertaking at my house. None of those tea bags for me. Those are for lazy folks, and for those who never learned to do it right. I take a handful of black tea, drop it into a pot of boiling water, and then move it to the back of the stove and let it steep for as long as it takes. After it sets there for two or three hours, you have to poke a hole in it to put the milk in, but a slug of that tea is more than a match for the chilblains.

Grover took off his mackinaw and hung it on the back of his chair, rolled up the ear tabs on his cap, sat down, and took a swig of that tea.

"I never drink tea but what I think of that fella over to Thorndike," Grover said. "Name was Fletcher Elkhorn, and I don't think he ever said more than a dozen words in the forty-odd years I knew him. He used to come into the snack bar every day around noon and order a cup of tea. Without fail, he would complain that it wasn't hot enough.

"Finally, one of the girls decided to see if she could make a cup of tea that would satisfy the old grouch, so around eleven-thirty one morning, she put the cup in the oven and baked it at three hundred degrees for half an hour. When the old man came in at noon, she poured boiling tea into that cup and served it to him. He took one sip of that brew, which must have burned his shoe taps, but he would not admit that he had been taken. He just looked at her and said, 'The Fool Killer will be coming to get you tomorrow.'"

While Grover was unlacing his rubber boots, I went to the window to check the thermometer.

"I must be getting old," I said. "It's only eight below zero, but it feels more like forty below."

"It's the wind," Grover said. "Good thing we don't get wind in the winter like some of them summer hurricanes. Hurricane Carol really raised the Old Harry around here. I remember I had a hen at the time. She was laying into the wind, and it blew so hard that she laid the same egg five times."

"Yup, I remember that one," I said. "It was some nasty. It blew so hard 'round here that the wind unraveled a crowbar. Matter of fact, one gust was so strong it blew two rooster feathers right through my grindstone."

🌲🌲🌲

"Another cup of tea, Grover?"

"Might as well," he said. "It's always a long evening when you get started on them weather yarns."

Grover is chief engineer on the tugboat *Half Moon* based out of Belfast. Having spent most of his adult life on the sea, I knew he enjoyed both telling and hearing weather tales, so, ignoring his remark, I began in earnest.

"My grandfather, Captain Orrin Hathaway," I began, "was in the three-masted schooner *Emily Beal* back in the day. This was, oh, maybe sixty or seventy years ago. Her home port was Portland, and she was three days overdue with a cargo of codfish from off the Grand Banks. They were two days from port when the wind just died right out and she just sat there. She was loaded to the deadeyes, wallowing in the trough, and slatting her gear to pieces with her cargo in danger of rotting in the hold.

"Old Captain Orrin put up with this for a bit, but he finally reached the end of his rope. He began to walk the quarterdeck and swear. He knew more cusswords than any Nova Scotia sailor I ever met, and, as you know, those Nova Scotia boys are champion blasphemers. After about twenty minutes of uttering obscenity after obscenity, he took out a silver dollar, held it up, and, addressing all the gods who might be on duty, he cried out, 'Damn it all, sell me some wind, will you?'

"He then threw that dollar coin high into the air, and it had no more than hit the water when the wind began to blow a living judgment. It was blowing some fierce. The wind took the masts, sails, and rigging over the side and turned the lifeboats into useless pieces of wood. The gale eventually drove her ashore just south of Cape Elizabeth, where she pounded herself to kindling in the surf and ledges. The whole crew made it ashore somehow, and after they got their bearings, one of them said, 'Well, Skipper, looks like you got your wind!'

"Looking at the remains of his ship and cargo, the old man just said, 'Yes—but if I'd known the wind was so cheap, I wouldn't have ordered quite so much.'"

A long silence followed while Grover stirred his third cup of tea. Finally, he looked me right in the face and eyes and said, "If I owed the Devil a thousand liars, and he wouldn't take you as a down payment, I'd think him a hard one to deal with."

We didn't say a word for a minute or two. Grover leaned forward to sip a little more of his tea, then pushed back in his chair and started in with another story.

"Back when I was captain of the *Explorer,*" he said. "I was just hanging around the dock one day when this beautiful yacht came steaming into the harbor.

"The captain tied up and come ashore, and I was the first one he bumped into. He was complaining that this yacht he had bought and paid a fortune for didn't seem to have no sense of direction—he couldn't get from one place to another on it without fetching up somewheres else. Well, he explained exactly what was happening, and of course, I knew right away what the problem was.

"See, they put the compass in the boat and then, when they put the engine in the boat, they didn't bother to calibrate the compass. That great mass of iron was drawing the compass way off course.

"So I told him, I said, 'Well, that's not a big problem. I know exactly what it is.'

"He says, 'Well, why don't you show me what the problem is.'

"Down off Rockland, in them days, the navy had set up these two trial buoys, exactly one mile apart on an exact heading, so what you do is, you steam back and forth between them two buoys and you adjust the adjusters on the compass until it reads exactly what the chart says it should read.

"Well, we got halfway down there, and all of a sudden the fog came rolling in, thick as three in a bed. Penobscot Bay is a shipping channel, and some of the vessels going up and down there are eight thousand feet long. Huge tankers.

"This guy got really excited; you see, the fog was so thick, you couldn't see the bow.

"He said, 'What are we gonna do? If the compass is no good, we don't know which way to head. We could run right into the side of one of them big ships, turn us right into kindlin' wood, and they wouldn't even know we'd hit 'em.'

"I says, 'Oh, no, no—when it's foggy like this and you don't know where you're headed, you navigate with potatoes.'

"Well, he looked at me like I was nuts, and he says, 'Navigate with potatoes? How the hell do you navigate with potatoes?'

"It's Downeast radar," I explained to him. "What you do is, you take a bag of them potatoes you got down below, you go up on the bow, and, one at a time, you throw 'em out ahead of you as hard as you can drive 'em, and when one of 'em don't splash, you turn."

🌲🌲🌲

"Speaking of lies," I said. "My great-uncle Curt always insisted that he met up with a timber rattler up in Washington County many years ago. The way he used to tell it was this:

"I was just getting ready to shove off, and I had everything I needed loaded into the canoe, when I noticed that I had forgotten the bait. Well, here I am, miles from any place where I could get bait and wondering what to do about it. While I'm pondering the situation, I happened to look down, and there in the underbrush was a big rattler with a frog in its mouth.

"Of course, frogs are excellent bait, but I really didn't want to take it away from the snake, so I took a jug of hard cider and poured some of it on that snake's head. It dropped the frog, and crawled off into the bushes. Well, I puttered around some, finished loading the gear and all, and I was just about to step into the canoe when I felt something hit my boot. I looked down and there was that snake, back with three more frogs!

" 'Uncle!' I said. 'Everyone knows that timber rattlers have been extinct in Maine for two hundred years. That must have been the last of its kind.'

"All Uncle Curt said was, 'No wonder it had a drinking problem.'"

🌲🌲🌲

"Speaking of drinking problems, Grover, I've got about five gallons of hard cider left over from last fall," I said. "Would you like a little snort of it?"

"I certainly would," he answered. "But I hope it's better than that last batch you made. One swallow of that would make you walk a barbed-wire fence barefoot with a wildcat under each arm."

By the time I returned from the cellar with the cider, Grover was waiting with a big tumbler.

"You know," he said. "There is something about hard cider and fishing trips. They just naturally go together. While you were down cellar, I got to thinking about that fishing trip up to Bear Brook. It's been all of thirty years now, but by gorry, that was a big trout I caught. When I pulled that fish out of the water, it took a full twenty minutes for the hole it left to fill back in again."

🌲🌲🌲

About that time my old grandfather clock struck nine.

"That old clock is nice to have around," Grover said, "but it keeps reminding folks that time keeps moving even when we don't want it to. My father used to tell about a lobster fisherman down to Cundy's Harbor who had an old grandfather clock for years. Kept perfect time, but one night it went haywire and struck fourteen times. The old man jumped up out of his easy chair and said to his wife, 'By thunder, let's get to bed; I've never known it to be so late!'"

🌲🌲🌲

With that Grover pulled on his boots and mackinaw and headed for the door.

"You don't have to rush on my account," I said. "It's only nine o'clock."

"Got to get a good night's sleep. Tomorrow we are going to work on the engine in the tugboat. Ever since we pulled that yacht off Hog Island bar last summer, she has been vibrating somethin' awful. I think we must have hit bottom and maybe chipped the wheel. Ever since then the stuffing box keeps leaking, so something must be out of true down there. Never could figure why they were anywhere near that bar in the first place. The captain, if you can call him that, said that some clam digger told him there was plenty of water in there. I told him, 'Sure there is, but it's just spread kinda thin in spots.' He had no sense of humor at all, so when I handed him a bill for towing, I also gave him a copy of Lindsey's Law for future reference."

Lindsey's Law simply states: When your draft exceeds the depth of the water, you are most assuredly aground.

"Glad you dropped in, Grover," I said as he was leaving. "Bring the wife next time. Watch yourself going down them steps; damned gutter leaked during that mild spell and its glare ice clear to the road."

Chapter 2

Town Characters

L ike I said earlier, ours is a town full of characters and stories. We've got way more than our fair share of both—always have, always will. You can find them across town, down the street, or right next door. Although, some of the "characters" I've known are long since dead, but so long as we remember them, I guess they will never be completely gone. At least I hope not. Their wit and wisdom live on, and the lives of those who remember them are enriched from having known them. Let me introduce you to a few.

Great-Uncle Curt

When you start talking about liars and storytellers, my Great-Uncle Curt runs full bore to the top of the list. He told so many stories and so many tall tales that someone once gave him a special trophy honoring him as the world's greatest liar. He displayed it over the fireplace with great pride. With Uncle Curt you never knew where the truth ended and the story began. He lived a long time and he saw a lot of things and he knew a lot of people. In addition to stories about his own adventures, he would often sit on the front porch and talk about the people who used to live in town back in the day.

Take Clarence Rich, for example. One day the old fella decided to shingle his roof. Somehow, he got his bundle of shingles, hauled over his ladder, and climbed up on the roof to work. At the time, he was not a day short of eighty-seven years old. Well, there he was up there just shingling away and somehow he lost his footing. He slid down them shingles, fell off the roof, and landed right in the middle of a manure pile. The boys raced over, gathered him up, and then cleaned him up a bit. Turns out he wasn't really hurt that bad, because luckily, so to speak, he landed in something quite soft.

Anyway, one of the boys says to him, "When you fell off of that roof, did your whole life pass before your eyes?"

Clarence looked right at him with bemused look on his face and said, "Of course not. I'm eighty-seven. I only fell ten feet!"

True, Uncle Curt was known to stretch the truth on occassion. I remember when I was a boy, he still owned one of those old long Spanish-American War rifles. It took a bullet about six inches long—or seemed like it. He'd always brag about that old rifle and what a good shot he was with it. On more than one occassion I heard him say that his aim was so good and that old rifle would shoot so far, that when he was hunting deer, he had to put salt on the bullet so the meat wouldn't spoil before he could get to it.

🌲🌲🌲

Uncle Curt was not just a great hunter, he was also one of the all-time great fisherman. One time he said he was out fishing for trout. Now anyone knows that a brook trout is a fish that is typically fairly small. In fact, the biggest one I have ever caught weighed maybe a pound or so soaking wet. But Uncle Curt was a superior fisherman is all regards and possessed a keen ability to find the big ones. One day he was fishing downeast when he caught a trout so big it nearly hauled him right out of the boat. Biggest one he ever caught, he said. Given its size, Uncle Curt wanted to know how much it weighed for braggin' purposes, so they hauled it into Machias, but unfortunately coudn't find a fish scale large enough to weigh it. Luckily, he did find a camera and took a picture as proof of his catch. He never did get an actual weight, but that fish was so big the picture negative alone weighed 14 pounds.

🌲🌲🌲

Another time Uncle Curt was up to camp with a green-horn hunter. This guy was right out of the middle of New York City, and had never been in Maine before. He was scared half to death of getting eaten up by some side-hill gouger, a tree squeak, or some other horrible creature that we'd told him about.

Anyway, it was some dark about ten that night when Uncle Curt told him it was the custom for the newest member of the party to get a pail of water from the spring for morning coffee. The last thing in the world that New Yorker wanted to do was to venture outside the camp at night and into the pitch black woods. However, he knew if he refused, he would never live it down, so he grabbed the bucket and headed out the door.

A couple of minutes later, he came busting back into the camp all feather-white and out of breath. His eyes looked like two boiled onions, and Uncle Curt said he never saw anyone so terrified in his life.

"What in Tophet ails you?" Uncle Curt asked, figuring the man had probably heard a noise he couldn't identify.

Finally, when the New Yorker had recovered enough wind to speak, he stammered, "There's a huge black bear standing in the water!"

Uncle Curt and the rest of the boys had a good laugh and finally said to him, "Well, don't you know that bear is just as afraid of you as you are of him?"

"Well, if that's true," he said. "Then that water ain't fit to drink anymore anyway."

🌲🌲🌲

Back in the old days when such descriptions were not considered inappropriate, Uncle Curt told me there was a man in town that everyone considered the town drunk. For years and years, all he did was hang around and drink. Still, he was harmless enough and everybody liked him and kinda looked after him, which was the Maine way.

As he got older, he told anyone who would listen that he only had one request: "When I die," he said, "I don't want you to bury me. I got a mortal fear of being buried alive. I want you to cremate me."

Everyone should shook their head in agreement. Cremation would save a lot of bother anyway.

Well, time went on, and, of course, the man eventually did die, drinking right to the bitter end. Everyone in town got together and agreed the proper thing to do was honor his last request, so they cremated him. Problem was it took a full three days to put the fire out.

🌲🌲🌲

Uncle Curt also used to plague his wife somethin' awful and she had no sense of humor at all. I heard him say one time: "She's so damned ugly, I take her everywhere I go."

"Well, that don't make no sense," someone said. "If she's so ugly, why don't you just leave her at home?"

"Well," Uncle Curt said. "I'd rather take her with me than have to kiss her good-bye."

🌲🌲🌲

There was a farmer who lived just over the hill from Uncle Curt. One day the farmer was out plowing his field with his famous prized breeding bull. Uncle Curt happened to come along and see what the farmer was doing and thought it odd. Not only was this a valueable breeding bull, but Uncle Curt knew for a fact that the farmer owned a brand new tractor that was just sitting idle in the barn. Curiousity got the best of him, so he went up to the farmer and asked him straight out: "Given that you have a new tractor in the barn, why in tarnation are you plowing your fields with your prized breeding bull?"

The old farmer stopped and looked over at Uncle Curt and said, "I want the old son of a bitch to know that life is not all just fun and games."

🌲🌲🌲

Like many of his generation, Uncle Curt was a very practical man. He heated his house with an ancient, wood-fired furnace, and he wasn't too fussy about what he burned in it. He used to reason, "If it's wood, it'll burn."

One time, he said he was driving along and saw a big pile of slabs beside the road. Of course, he was interested to know if they were for sale, so he pulled into the driveway, walked up to the house, and knocked on the door.

An old man opened the door, and Curt asked him the price of them slabs. The old fella says, "Let me put it this way—the more you take, the less it will cost you."

Will and Eula

Everyone agrees that honesty is the best policy, but there are times when even honesty has a price, as in the case of my neighbors, Will and Eula.

Will, as I recall, was on his death bed and Eula was by his side for quite a while. At one point he opened his eyes and said "I gotta confess something. I may not make it and I gotta tell ya, I've been unfaithful. And every time I was unfaithful, I cut a notch in the back of the grandfather clock—all three times."

Eula was silent for a minute and the she replied: "Well, that you for being honest. I guess I also should confess that I was unfaithful too. And every time I was I put a bean in that gallon jug in the pantry, and they're all there, except the five quarts I took to church suppers over the years."

William Carpenter

The old-time Mainer has always been known for being practical, a bit frugal and tight with a dollar. One of the best stories I know to illustrate this is the tale Uncle Curt told me about two old farmers, William Carpenter and Jim Ford. One fall, both of the farmers went to the county fair and proceeded to eat more than their fair share of fried food. As luck would have it, they were both stricken with the need to go to the privy at the same time.

This was back in the day and they went into one of them long privies that had more than one hole. When they both had finished what they was there for, William stood up, and when he did, the spare change that was in his pocket fell out and dropped right down the hole. He stood there for a minute just staring back down the hole where he had just been sitting. Finally, he started taking off his shoes, his overalls, his shirt, and so forth until he was buck naked.

Jim just stood there, somewhat dumbfounded.

William then grabbed his pants, reached in the pocket and took out a five dollar bill which he promptly dropped down the hole.

That was just too much for Jim.

"Have you gone crazy?" he blurted out. "What on earth did you do that for?"

William paused for a minute.

"Crazy?" he questioned. "You don't think I'm goin' down there just to get a handful of change, do ya?"

Another time, during a particularly long and hot dry spell, the same William Carpenter noticed that his water was starting to taste kind of funny. Most of the other wells in town had dried up, so he was feeling kinda fortunate. But after a few days with no improvement in taste, he decided he should get the water tested. He gathered up a water sample and sent it off to the state lab for testing.

As soon as the state tested that water, they called him right up and said, "Don't use any more of that water. We are sending an inspector to your property to see what is going on."

The next day the inspector comes out and looks at the property. He notices that the well is awful close to the cesspool. After he finishes the inspection, he tells the farmer, "Look you have a choice here: either you can stop using the cesspool or you can stop drinking the water."

The farmer decided since they still had an old outhouse and they really couldn't go without water, they would stop using the cesspool. So, that's what he did, he stopped using the cesspool and I'll be damned, but two days later the well dried up.

Cecil Davis

Cecil Davis, an old friend of mine from back home, came up from Milbridge to live in Portland, and he got a job as a city bus driver. Well, he's a typical Downeaster—he don't take no guff off of nobody.

One day he pulls up to a bus stop on Congress Street, opens the door, and there's a guy standing there with a Great Dane dog. It was a huge dog. Well, Cecil looked at the guy, looked at the dog, and says, "You can't bring that dog on the bus."

Well, you know how some people are about their dogs, the guy responds, "Well, I guess you know where you can stick your bus."

Cecil didn't miss a beat.

"Ayuh," he said. "And if you can do the same thing with that dog, you can get on this bus."

Another time a passenger got on the bus just to take a scenic tour around Portland.

This fella was visiting from Texas. You know how it is in Texas—everything's bigger and better.

So, the Texan says, "What's that building over there?"

Cecil says, "That's City Bank. That building is one of the biggest in all of Maine."

"Seriously?" scoffed the Texan. "Why, man, down in Texas, we've got outhouses bigger than that!"

"Ayuh," Cecil says. "I guess prob'ly you need 'em."

Joe Perham

One day I was headed up to visit my old friend Joe Perham in West Paris. I was taking the "scenic" route and driving some back country roads. I was driving along probably going 30 or 35 miles per hour when all of a sudden a chicken ran right past me like I was anchored. I was mighty curious, so I sped up and when I got close enough—by this time I was doing almost 60—I saw that this chicken had four legs. Four legs! Maybe a half mile later, the chicken turned into a long driveway and raced off. Curiosity got the best of me and I turned down the driveway to see where it was going. At the end of the driveway, I saw an old farmer by the pig pen. I stopped and asked him where on earth he got a four-legged chicken.

"Well," said the farmer. "Every Sunday I kill a chicken for supper. My wife and I both like the drumsticks best and one drumstick each just ain't enough for a Sunday meal. So, one day I had the bright of idea of breeding a chicken with four legs so that we could have more drumsticks. And I'll be darned, if it didn't work."

"Impressive," I said. "That's quite a feat. But, just curious, can you taste the difference?"

"Don't know," said the farmer. "Can't catch one."

🌲🌲🌲

Well, I was still shaking my head at the thought of a four-legged chicken when I got to Joe's farm and right there in the yard was a pig with a wooden leg—It was very peculiar. I asked Joe what the story was behind the pig with the wooden leg.

"Well," says Joe. "Funny thing about that pig. I was plowing down in the back field and my tractor hit a hole and flipped over. The darn thing pinned me right to the ground. I couldn't get clear of it, so I started hollering for help. That pig, back then he still had four good legs, heard me and I'll be darned but he didn't come running down the field. He rooted around by my side and dug a ditch beside me. He rolled me into the ditch, grabbed my pantleg in his mouth and just hauled me right out. I was some grateful."

"That's unbelieveable," I said. "But that can't be why he has a wooden leg?"

"No, no, I'm getting to that," he said. "It wasn't but a few weeks ago that my little grandson was playin' in the road and one of them huge pulp wood trucks came tearing down the road headed right for him. Suddenly, that pig, still with four good legs, busted out of his pen, ran into the road, grabbed the boy by the shirttail and dragged him to safety."

"That's amazing," I said. "But I still don't understand why he is hobbling around on a wooden leg?"

"Well," he said. "You get a nice faithful animal like that, and you don't just eat him all at once."

Travis Smith

There was this young fella named Travis Smith—I guess you could say he weren't wrapped very tight, or, my favorite, he weren't threaded all the way on.

Well, he got to hanging out with this woman, and his father got kinda put out with him, because he was kinda numb. He was spending all his time with this woman and he wasn't working or wasn't paying to any attention of his other responsibilities.

His father says, "Son, don't you know that that girl has been with every man in town?"

The boy looked at him and said, in her defense "Well, the town ain't that big."

🌲🌲🌲

A short while later, Travis was telling that story to one of his friends.

"I guess dad's right," he said. "But she ain't the only one. You know after I started thinking about it, I guess I've probably have been with every woman in town except my mother and my sister."

His friend just shook his head slowly, "Well, that's probably about right. But if it makes you feel any better, I can tell you for a fact that you ain't missing much."

Rev. MacDonald

Back years ago there was a preacher, Rev. MacDonald, and he was good friends with Vincent Smith, a local farmer. They got together and socialized and discussed everything under the sun.

Vincent bought a donkey for the kids to play with, and they rode that thing all over the yard and the fields and had a grand old time.

One day Rev. MacDonald came to visit, and they were discussing everything, including that donkey.

"You know," said Rev. MacDonald. "I've noticed that every time you refer to that animal there, you call it a donkey. Now, the Good Book says that animal is an ass. Perfectly respectable word, used in the right context."

"You know, you're right," Vincent said. "I never thought of that."

Well, from that day on Vincent referred to the animal by its proper name, the ass.

Of couse, one day the animal died, and the farmer was out, digging it a grave. He only brought up two or three shovelfuls of dirt when the minister come 'round the corner of the barn. He looked and he says, "What are you doing, digging a post hole?"

"No," Vincent said. "I'm . . . er . . . well, matter of fact . . . er . . . I'm digging a donkey hole."

Judge Coffin

You've all probably heard me talk about Uriah Boardman. Well, one time he decided that he'd never done anything that anyone would notice, so he made up his mind to do something that nobody would ever forget. And, he did just that. At the age of eighty-seven, he decided to go streaking.

Ayuh. Streaking.

One Friday morning he went down to the town hall. He picked a great time and a great location. It was a public place, and on this particular day they were hosting a big spring flower show. He waited out back and kept peekin' in the windows. He wanted to pick a time that would maximize his exposure, so to speak.

When he got ready, he peeled off all of his clothes, except for his shoes, and he went running right through that flower show. (He thought he was running; actually, he was just jogging.)

Anyway, the Dunbar sisters was there, Emma and Effie, and they were just squirting a little water on their prize rose. Well, Emma saw him go by out 'round the corner, right by this big fern. She says to Effie, "Lord, lord, Effie, did you see that? What was that man wearing?"

Effie says, "I don't know, but it needs pressin'."

Somebody called the police and about ten minutes later, a couple of young cops landed there. Of course, they didn't have any trouble catchin' Uriah—they just grabbed him by the begonias and hauled him straight into court.

Well, Judge Coffin was some wild. See, he and Uriah were the same age. They grew up together, and I guess the judge was afraid he might be losing his own marbles. He fined Uriah all he could—he even tacked on another ten dollars (called it a moving violation). He fined him thirty-five dollars, all told.

Well, down there in them days, you paid your fine right there to the clerk in front of the judge. There's Uriah standing there, peeling one-dollar bills off this roll he liked to carry, and he's grinning like a dog eating bumblebees.

Judge Coffin got even madder.

The Judge says, "You cussed old fool—you've been arrested, you've been fined, you're gonna have a police record—what is the matter with you? You ought to be ashamed of yourself. Now I want to know, what's so cussed funny?"

Uriah kept right on counting. He says, "Well, Judge, I'll tell ya—I reckon' it has all worked out to the good, seeing as I won $50 for Best Dried Arrangement."

🌲🌲🌲

Old Judge Coffin was not afraid to go hard on people in his court if he felt it necessary.

One time this old fella, Joseph Farley was fishing without a license. The local police had caught him down in the brook a few times and let him off with just a warning each time. Finally, they had had enough and hauled him into court in front of Judge Coffin who, because of all the warnings, fined him a whopping $50 dollars. Old Joseph wasn't too pleased. So as he was paying the fine, he asked the judge for a receipt.

Judge Coffin said, "Sure, you can have a receipt, but what's the matter—don't you trust us?"

The old fella looked the judge right in the eye and said, "Oh, sure, I trust you Judge, but you and I are getting along in years now, and before too long we are both going to be meeting our maker.

"Well, when I get to the pearly gates, St. Peter is going to ask me if I have ever committed a crime, and I'll have to say 'Yes.' Then he's going to ask if I have ever been to court, and I'll have to say 'Yes.' Then he will ask if I paid my fine, and if I don't have that receipt as proof, they are going to be looking all over hell for Judge Coffin."

Emma and Effie Dunbar

The Dunbar sisters, Emma and Effie, lived on the old family homestead for all their lives. Neither one of them got married. In fact, neither one had ever had a boyfriend—not even one date. I guess their mother, who was well known to be a bitter toward life, told them her version of the facts of life, and it scarred them two sisters so bad, they decided they wanted nothing to do with men. Nothing at all. In fact, they had this old female cat for a pet, and they wouldn't even let that poor cat out, for the same reason.

Anyway, as I say, that went on for years. It got to the point where they wouldn't even let the milkman come up on the porch to deliver the mail—they made him leave it at the mailbox down at the end of the road.

The years went by, and by some strange twist of fate, very late in life, Emma met a man. They courted for a bit and then she actually got married. After the wedding, the newlyweds left on their honeymoon which they spent at a nice romantic inn down by the ocean.

It wasn't but two days after the honeymoon started that Effie got a postcard from Emma. All it said was *Let the cat out!*

🌲🌲🌲

Poor old Effie, after Emma got married, she was kinda lonesome kicking around the old homestead—nobody there but herself and that cat (who did seem in better spirits, I might add).

Anyway, Effie decided that she was going to splurge on herself for once and get a new privy. I used to build privies, so she hired me to come build her one. I didn't really want to, because I knew that Effie was a taskmaster and anything less than perfection was not gonna do.

But I had no choice—I needed the money, so I went over and I built her the best privy I'd ever built. Took special pains with it. Why, I even papered the inside of it—nice pattern I thought she'd like. I looked that privy all over and decided it had my stamp of approval.

Two days later I got a note from Effie with no money in the envelope. There was just a note from her saying, *I ain't paying, and I ain't saying why.*

Well, I knew there was something seriously wrong with that privy. I also knew I was going to have to find it. She ain't about to discuss privies with me.

When I got the chance, I went over. I looked it all over, and couldn't see anything wrong with it. Door was pinched a little bit, but that wasn't it. I looked up under the eaves because I thought there might be a hornets' nest. Nothing. Went inside, looked all around—I thought, maybe a spider-web. Nothing. It all looked perfect.

Well, I got desperate, because I knew there was something wrong with that new privy, and finally, like anybody would—out of desperation, you know—I stuck my head down the hole, 'cause I didn't know what I was looking for, or where to find it.

Well, wouldn't you know it? I'd no more than got my head down that hole when she stepped into that privy behind me. I was startled and embarrassed. I yanked my head up out of that hole, and when I did, one of my whiskers caught in a crack in that seat.

"Ouch," I cried out.

"There," she said. "Smarts, don't it?"

Chapter 3

At the Maine Drag Diner

"Nothin' ever changes around here," Uncle Warren said. "I believe that the Law of Inertia was passed in this town. Nothin' has really changed here in the last thirty years, except for all them hippies comin' here, thinkin' they were gonna get back to the land. They got some big surprise when they found out that the land didn't want 'em back."

Uncle Warren (actually, he's not really an uncle to anyone, but nearly everyone in town calls him uncle out of respect) was holding court as usual in Ruby Collins's Maine Drag Diner. This ritual has been going on every Saturday for the last ten years or so. That was just about the time he lost his wife and spending Saturday nights at the diner is one way he has been dealing with the loneliness of being a widower with no children.

Uncle Warren is about seventy years old. No one knows for sure his exact age, and if you ask him, he will simply say,

"Old enough to know the score, but still young enough to play the game."

He's a genuine old Maine character who always wears long underwear, flannel shirts, and an outdated necktie the year 'round. He can be found sitting in the same booth, the one with a big piece of Formica missing, as regular as the tides.

He's always clean-shaven and neat, except for that necktie. I'm sure he hasn't untied it in years—he just keeps slipping the knot up and down to fit over his head. It's quite frayed now, and it's spotted with everything from dandruff to gravy from last Thanksgiving's turkey dinner.

Uncle Warren was born right here in town. He quit school in the eighth grade to go to work as a woodcutter, he has very little use for people with a formal education, and he is a staunch Republican. His large frame is still solid, even after years of retirement. He may be going bald, but we can't tell because he never removes his old hat. He has relatives down in Boston, and they keep inviting him to come visit, but he's not willing to give up being the weekly star, at least in his mind, of the Maine Drag Diner.

So now here it is Saturday night at the diner, and Uncle Warren is holding court. Again.

"Why," he went on, "they still only got a two-hole outhouse down to the Grange Hall—after all these years, the demand for larger accommodations just hasn't happened.

"And you take Ira Crabtree down to Crabtree's General Store, for example—he's been sellin' the same old stuff for years now, all the necessities—mousetraps, dishrags, cider vinegar, shotgun shells, and penny candy. Even he ain't ready for modern times yet. There's stuff in that store that should have been throwed out years ago. Why, he's still got two feed bags for sale, and there ain't been a workhorse around here for decades.

"Now, mind you, I don't favor change just for the sake of change. Our dirt roads are good enough—except maybe for the big rock in the middle of the Old Pond Road; no one would miss that if we did away with it, except maybe Pete Doughty, the mechanic down to the garage. He's made a fortune off summer people who run aground on it with their fancy, low-slung cars."

Settling back with another cup of black coffee, Uncle Warren continued with his observations on the absence of change in the town.

"I see in the papers that all them economists are predictin' another recession. So, what else is new? It's always a recession around here, and if it cost a dollar to go 'round the world, I couldn't get out of sight."

Warren paused for a moment, waiting for someone to laugh at that old saw, but no one did, so he pushed on.

"I started out sixty years ago with nothin'—still got most of it. I guess if you're a shopkeeper, it can be really difficult.

Ira Crabtree says that things have gotten so bad that even the people who don't pay their bills have stopped buying.

"I was talkin' to Ira just the other day, askin' him how business was, and he says, 'Well, it's like this: Last Monday I sold a nice sleeping bag to this fella from away. Tuesday, I didn't sell nothing. Wednesday, the fella from away came back and returned the sleeping bag. So I guess Tuesday has been my best day.'

"He ain't kiddin' anyone anyway. He likes it slow. I recall one time I was in his store and he was playin' checkers with Uriah Boardman. This summer complaint came in and wanted to buy some sugar. Ira says: 'Ain't got any. Don't carry it no more. Sells so fast I can't keep it in stock.'

"Nope," Uncle Warren went on, "I'm afraid the only ones doin' any real business around here are the grocery stores and the fuel oil dealers. Some of the boys are sellin' firewood to folks who think they are gonna save money on heat, but even wood is too high. In fact, if it goes any higher, I'm gonna be tempted to do what Abner Larrabee says he did back durin' the Great Depression. Claims he kept warm all winter with just one stick of firewood—he kept throwin' it out the window and then goin' out after it."

While Uncle Warren paused to get his second wind, I decided to throw out something just to see how he would react.

"You know that back in the old days," I said, "people got what they wanted by the barter system. Seems to me that if it worked then, it ought to work now."

"Barter!" Warren spat that word out like it was lima beans, or something equally disgusting. "You talk like one of them darn hippies. That foolishness may have worked in the old days, but since they invented money, most people won't settle for anything else.

"Besides, it's already been tried lately. A couple of years ago Leonard Wormwood, the dairy farmer, and Maynard Philbrook, the woodcutter, thought they'd try it. Maynard had plenty of wood, but he needed milk for those eight kids of his. Leonard had plenty of milk but needed firewood. The two of them jawed and dickered for a while, but they couldn't decide on how much wood was worth how much milk, so they gave it up and went back to usin' money. Only trouble is, they still have too much milk and wood, and neither of them has much money. Nope, I'm afraid money has become a necessity of life, even for them that don't have any."

By this time Ruby Collins, owner of the diner, was making frequent trips to our table, asking if we wanted anything else. She has little patience for these Saturday-night gatherings of town characters, but she puts up with it some-how, even though not much food is bought.

Ruby works long hours. She is thin, stooped, and never smiles. Years ago a young man jilted her and ran off to Philadelphia with a younger woman. Neither of them ever came back to town again, and no one ever mentions them while Ruby is around. It hit her pretty hard, I guess. Ever since her opinion of most men can be guessed at by the sign over the coffeemaker, which reads: THE MORE I SEE OF MEN, THE MORE I LIKE MY CAT.

It was obvious that she wanted to clear the tables and make room for other customers, but either Uncle Warren didn't notice, or he chose not to see. Lighting his foul-smelling pipe, he was soon off on another tirade.

"I see on the warrant for Town Meeting that some quill-head wants to have a white line painted down the center of the Skunk Hollow road. That's crazy! They'd have to widen the road first. 'Taint much wider than a paintbrush now.

"It's probably them same clowns that voted to make Morning Street one-way that time. Whoever heard of makin' a dead-end street one-way? Everyone who lives on the other end would have been stuck there and couldn't git back. Seems to me that you are just askin' for this kind of mess when you elect a man who has ten kids to the planning board."

Although Warren does tend to stretch the truth a tad, he has a point. Many people are moving into Maine from big cities, trying to get away from big government, high taxes, and crime. When they get here, they jump in with both feet trying to make it just like the place they escaped from.

"About two years ago, this couple from New Jersey moved up here by way of Boston," Uncle Warren recalled. "Quite well off in everything except common sense. You know the type: They drive a Volvo, buy expensive organic food, worship the earth, and listen to nothing but NPR.

"Well, he—Foster Pickering—is an investment broker who commutes to Boston. Only comes home on weekends, so his wife, Elizabeth—better known 'round here as Miss Picky—has nothin' to do but meddle in town affairs and raise Afghan hounds. Funniest-looking dogs I ever seen. They look like worn-out dust mops on a hunger strike. Good for nothin', far as I can see. If anyone is goin' to have a hound, why not a beagle or coon hound? What do you hunt with an Afghan hound?

"Anyway, she'd barely been here for one whole day when she started tryin' to change things. Right after they moved in, she loaded up the car with all the leftover boxes and other cultch and headed for the dump. 'Bout two hours later she found it. Well, she was some put out from spendin' her valuable time ridin' around huntin' for the dump, so she said to Old Tom, the dump tender, 'Why don't you put up a sign so people can find this place?'

"Old Tom looked her right in the face and eyes and he said, 'Don't need to advertise—got all the business I want.'

"Of course, he's had run-ins with summer people before— you prob'ly heard 'bout the time some summer complaint arrived at the dump with a whole station wagon full of trash, and Tom just stood there and watched her unload it. I guess she must have thought he was supposed to help her, but he never lifted a finger. When she was finished and ready to go, she was some huffy with him, and she says, 'You know, mister, there are a lot of odd-acting people in this state.'

" 'Ayuh,' Tom says, 'but most of them are gone by Labor Day.'"

🌲🌲🌲

Storytellers are all alike. One tale leads to another, and the original subject—in this case, Town Meeting—usually gets misplaced. At least for a while.

Ruby is back, hovering over our table, and I'm feeling like someone ought to leave and start a mass exodus, but Uncle Warren is off again, and it wouldn't be polite to walk out while someone is talking. Problem is, he's always talking.

"I got laid off one winter a few years ago, and I was workin' with Ralph, the road commissioner, plowin' snow and sanding the roads. This particular day we were plowing out the Back Narrows road, and, at the same time, spreadin' sand as we went. For about two miles there had been a little sports car followin' us and tryin' to pass. Well, he kept gittin' more and more impatient all the time, and finally, he saw half a chance to pass, and away he went. Guess he didn't realize that we were clearin' the road, and once he got by us it was all glare ice. Cussed fool got right alongside us and gunned it, spun around a couple of times, and plowed right into the side of our truck. I'm tellin' you, he was some huffy.

"We stopped, and this fool jumped up on the runnin' board, looked Ralph dead in the eye, and yelled: 'I want to see your driver's license!'

"Ralph, he don't get excited too easy, he just says, 'In this state you don't need a license to get run into.'"

🌲🌲🌲

Uncle Warren looked around to see where Ruby was, but she was busy at another table, so he took advantage of the lull and continued.

"Town Meeting—all they ever do is argue and spend money. It don't hardly seem worth the bother, but once in a while it can be interesting. One time Miss Picky was all in a lather about snowplowin', or the lack of it. Her road is always one of the last to get plowed, and when she first moved here, she made a fuss at Town Meeting. Ralph always plows the main roads first, so the fire truck and school bus can get out, and then he plows the side roads and, finally, the newest roads where the new people live. Seems they like the dirt roads and livin' in the woods, but in the wintertime, it's not that great.

"Anyhow, she was all fired up about the poor service they were gittin' out her way, so she asked what it said in Ralph's contract about plowin'. Talk about surprised when she found out that he didn't have a contract! She got all haired up and says, 'What—no contract! Good grief, what if he just decides one day that he doesn't want to plow? He's not bound legally without a contract. This is incredible! How long has he been working without a contract?'

"Elmer, the first selectman, he turns to Sam, second selectman, and he says, 'Is this Ralph's twenty-ninth or thir-tieth year?'

"When the laughter died down she was a lot less visible."

"Speaking of Miss Picky," Stan Pinkham said, "I won-der if she and her husband ever came to realize what Curtis Campbell did to them in the cow deal?"

Stan hadn't said a word all evening, and for minute or so, no one knew what he was talking about. He began to explain.

"When they first came here, they decided to get a cow and be part-time farmers. Really get back to the land, you might say. Of course, they didn't know any more about cows than they did about dogs, so when Curtis offered to sell them his cow, they jumped on it. Don't you remember that old bony thing he had? Been dry for years, but he just didn't have the heart to do away with her, but he couldn't really afford to keep over the winter. Anyway, he told them that the cow had been bred—he didn't say which year—and if she didn't deliver a calf in the spring, he would refund every cent they paid for her.

"Naturally, the following spring there was no sign of a calf, so, true to his word, he gave back all the money they had paid for her. Well, coming from New Jersey, they had never seen a word-of-mouth contract honored like that, and they told him how much they appreciated his honesty and all . . . What they didn't realize was that they had fed his useless old cow all winter *for nothing!*"

If you sit by the window of the diner for a while on a Saturday evening, you will see just about everyone who lives in town. It's the only evening that the stores stay open late, so everyone who is able to get out does so on Saturday evening. It's rare to see Ernest Sprague out and about these days. At ninety-four, he seldom ventures out in the cold anymore, but, during a lull in the conversation, he happened to walk by the window, on his way to the drugstore.

Someone remarked that if Ernest didn't die this winter, they should bury him on suspicion. Another said that Ernest is so old, he won't buy green bananas.

Nothing ever gets by Uncle Warren, and when he saw Ernest walk by, he said, "Talk about coincidence! I was just now thinkin' of him and that time the hippies over behind the Old Pond Road put an article in the town warrant to get a bridge built across Beaver Road. Seems they like to jog and ride bicycles over the foot trail from Old Pond to the center of town.

"Now, that trail is older than Methuselah. And besides, there ain't more than a foot or two of water there. Anyway, this bunch of communists wanted the town to spend a bunch of money on a bridge so that they could get their exercise. Beats me why they didn't just build it themselves if they wanted exercise.

"Well, as I say, this bridge thing got on the warrant and word spread like cold sores. Every taxpayer in town was there to vote it down, except the hippies. Even Ernest was there, and he hadn't been to a Town Meeting in years. A man his age shouldn't get excited, but he was some het up over this one. He kept yelling out of turn, and the moderator kept orderin' him to sit down and keep quiet, but it didn't do much good.

"Finally Ernest saw a break, and he jumped up and yells, 'Damn it all! That brook ain't wide enough to put a bridge across—I could piss halfway cross't that brook!'

"Of course, the moderator was some put out with him by then, and he banged the table with his gavel and yelled, 'Mr. Sprague, you are out of order!'

"Didn't even slow the old boy down. Ernest yelled back, 'Yes, I know I am—if I wasn't, I could piss clear across't it!'

"Everyone just roared with laughter, except Ernest. He was so haired up he thought they were all laughing at *him* instead of what he'd said, so he left in a huff. Just as he got to the door he turned and bellowed, 'Town Meeting is supposed to be the truest form of democracy—but that's the trouble, *too damn many Democrats!*' "

🌲🌲🌲

"One other time, this was years ago, we had a town gravedigger named B.S. Phillips," Uncle Warren continued. "So, when Lucy Pratt died, it was his job to dig her grave. You probably don't remember Lucy, but her sister Vivian still lives on Morning Street, spry as ever at ninety-one. She was in the A&P last week asking Bill Grant the price of his pork chops. He quoted a price and she nearly fainted. She says,

'Accordin' to that, I've got a pig over to my place that's worth two thousand dollars!'

"Anyhow, B.S. dug Lucy's grave and gave his bill to the first selectman. Elmer looked at it and calmly reminded B.S. that the goin' rate for diggin' a grave was three dollars. B.S. insisted that it was worth five dollars, because of all the ledge he had to pound through. Elmer insisted that the town would not pay five dollars. Old B.S. shook his fist at Elmer and yelled, 'By thunder, if you don't give me five, up she comes!'

"B.S. wasn't a sentimental soul, anyway," Uncle Warren recalled. "I remember when his father died, he was headed for the graveyard with his pick and shovel. I said to him, 'Sorry to hear you are buryin' your father, Mr. Phillips.'

"He never even looked sideways when he said, 'Got to— he's dead.' "

Chapter 4

Father Fell Down the Well

One Saturday night at the Maine Drag Diner I took advantage of a lull in the conversation to jump in with a story of my own before Uncle Warren could get all revved up again.

"I will never forget," I said, "the year my father fell down the well. It was back in 1937 and I remember it was a Saturday night, on account the stores were open late. Mother and I drove into town to do the week's shopping. We ate early so's to get there by half past six, 'cause Mother always liked to sit and watch the train come in and see who got off.

"We left Father settin' in the kitchen, with his feet in the oven, reading *The Farm and Fireside*. We hadn't been gone very long when he heard an awful cackling out back in the henhouse. Somethin' had been getting the poultry all fall—about once a week, we'd been a hen short—but there was no sign of what done it, no tracks that we could see. Well, I figured it was probably a fox or a skunk, maybe even a weasel, but Father, he was certain it was a chicken thief. He loaded up his old Ithaca with a double handful of rock salt and he allowed that, sooner or later, the thief would come back, and he was really gonna season him.

"So, when he heard the hens cackling, he grabbed his shotgun and went out in the yard. Sure enough, by gorry, a fella come backing right out the henhouse with one of Mother's best Barred Rocks under his arm. Well, he should never have backed out. He didn't see Father at all, but he made an awful good target, and Father let him have it with both barrels. Got him right between the hip pockets.

"I guess that fella didn't do much sitting for a while—leastwise, not very comfortably. Turned out it was one of them thievin' Plourde boys that lived over behind the oil-cloth factory. He was into Doc Andrews's office next day, getting some of the salt picked out of him, and Doc said afterwards, 'If he had died, there was one end of him that wouldn't have to be embalmed, because it was so well salted.'

"Well, we finally found out what was happening to the hens, but that wa'nt nothing compared to what happened to Father. Ya see, when he fired, he was standin' right next to the well curb. Of course, the old gun kicked, so he stepped back to catch his balance, caught his heel on the well curb, and Father fell down the well.

"Mother and I got home pretty late, about eight o'clock, and after I'd unhitched and stabled Old Nellie, I brought the groceries into the kitchen.

"Mother says, 'I can't find your Father!'

"So we looked all around, and I noticed that the gun was gone from behind the door, and I figured that he'd gone hunting. Of course, it wasn't really legal to hunt before daybreak, but he always took a lantern along, and I once heard him say he'd never seen a deer wearing a watch.

"Well, when he didn't show up the next day, I asked around the General Store and the Farmers' Union, but no one 'round there had seen him. About a week later, we had a spell of Indian summer, and the water begun to taste funny.

"I said, 'Mother, I'll bet Father's down the well!'

"So I got a long piece of whipcord and a barn lantern, lowered it down the well, and, sure enough, there was Father. We couldn't just figure the best way to get him out, but it was okay, because we could still fetch water from the spring up on the ridge that fed the horse trough. That was always good 'til freeze-up time, so we was all set 'til well into November.

"A couple of days later I was out in the yard, splitting up some birch for the stove, when I noticed a rig coming out from town. I thought I recognized the mare, and, sure enough, when the fella turned into the yard, it was Reverend Eldridge.

"Now, I ain't got nothing against preachers as a breed, but Eldridge, he always rubbed me the wrong way. He was a regular fussbudget, worse than an old woman, and he could preach the longest of anyone I ever see. Worst thing about him, he had one of them thin, whiny voices, the kind that sets your teeth on edge. I can take a long sermon if I have to, but if there's one thing I can't abide, it's a whiner.

"He climbed down out of the buggy and just stood there, holding the horse with one hand and clawin' at his whiskers with the other.

"Finally he says, 'Well, I thought I'd come around and console ya a mite, seein' you've lost your father.'

"So I says, 'Hell, Reverend, we ain't lost Father—he's down the well!'

"He lit into me somethin' awful. Among other things, he said that failing to honor my father like I was doin' was a willful breaking of the Fifth Commandment. I told him that if I was gonna set out to break one of the Ten Commandments, I could find that was a lot more fun than the Fifth, and besides that, didn't the Good Book have anything to say about keepin' your nose out of other folks' business?

"Well, that really stirred him up, and he said that it was my bounden duty to get Father underground, and he aimed to see that I done it. Then he quoted some more Scriptures at me, said I was a lazy, good-for-nothin' pup, and an undutiful son to boot!

"Well, by that time I was madder than a hornet. I hadn't never hit a preacher—that is, not at that time—so I just muckled onto a dump cart full of dirt and gravel that was standin' in the driveway, upended it, and let the whole cussed mess rattle right down the well on top of Father!

"'There,' I says. 'Now Father's underground. Does that satisfy ya?'

"Well, it didn't. Why, he was so worked up, he liked to bust a gusset. He was all red in the face, waving both arms over his head. I thought he was goin' to strangle himself, tryin' to talk. He shook his fist under my nose and said that if I didn't get Father down to the cemetery, I ought to be horsewhipped, and he had half a mind to do it himself.

"I told him I didn't think he could whip a pint of cream with a barn shovel. I picked up my ax, waved it under his nose, and told him if he didn't want to go back to town a head shorter, he'd better pull foot while he was able. Guess he thought I meant it. Anyway, he got back into his rig and drove off toward town, whiter than a sheet.

"I calmed down pretty quick after that. Got to thinkin' about what he said—about the graveyard and all. Of course, he was right, really, but still—there was Father, down the well, under a yard of loam and kinda hard to get to!

"Now, our farm sets on the south side of Bee Ridge, and the land falls away to the south'ard, right down to the road where the cemetery is. So, what I finally done, I took a spade and a mattock, went down to the graveyard, and dug a nice hole, six by six by four, right square in the middle of the family plot. Then I dug a drain all the way up the rise, cross't the dooryard to the well curb, and, well, I guess Father ought to be pretty well dreened by now!"

Uncle Warren studied me for a few seconds and then said: "Captain, that's the damnedest lie you ever told! I happen to know that your father died in 1944, not 1937!"

Well, when you have been called a liar, there are two things you can do: Fight, or go home.

"Oh hell, it's late," I said, and got up to leave.

Chapter 5

Cheaper to Quit Smoking

The morning dawned clear and bitter cold again. Just as I was getting ready to knit some bait bags to sell to the local lobster fishermen, I realized that I was out of tobacco. Going all day without tobacco is like facing the grim specter of death to a half-and-half addict like me, so, in spite of the subzero weather, I fired up the car and headed down to Ira Crabtree's store.

I've always said that automobiles were no more designed for this bitter climate than humans, but with a new battery I had just bought, she fired up and got rolling much quicker than I did. Them people that's always lamenting the passing of the good old days never had to crank a Model T and then bundle up in a buffalo robe to keep from freezing to death while they rode two miles to the store.

About half a mile from the store, the engine just up and died on me. It was so cold that the automatic choke couldn't open, and she just flooded herself solid full of raw gas. While I was wondering how I was going to hold that choke open and turn the engine over at the same time, Junior Farnsworth came along, and, seeing the hood up, he figured something was wrong, so he stopped and wanted to know if I had a problem.

"If being stuck with a dead car at fourteen below zero, with arms six feet too short, is a problem, then yes," I said, "I do have a problem."

After we got her started again, Junior stuffed a screwdriver handle down in the carburetor and said I should leave it there until I got home. Folks say he is as numb as a pounded thumb, but he certainly does know something about cars.

"Them automatic chokes are just something else to frig up," he said. "If it was mine, I'd put a hand choke on her."

He looked quite puzzled when I said, "Maybe I'll just quit smoking, instead."

🌲🌲🌲

The store was full of idlers, as usual, all sitting in a circle around the big Station Agent stove, and the odor of over-heated wool clothes reminded me that some things never change. It was almost the same as when I first went there with my father many years ago. The minute we entered the store that day, old John Prince said to my father, "I'll give you two cents and a rusty fishhook for that boy."

It nearly scared me to death. He was so strange-looking, with his long white beard streaked with tobacco juice, and only one tooth in his head. I didn't know what to think when Father answered, "Daow, I wouldn't want to cheat you. Why, he ain't worth half that price."

Old John and a few others are gone, now, but the same old stories are still being told by old-timers who were teenagers in those days. While I was buying my tobacco, poor old Lizzie Gardner came in all haired up, and said to Ira, "I want to buy a mousetrap. Last night a mouse got into my drawers and chewed all the fringe off my center piece!"

The reaction over by the stove started as a snicker, but soon they were all roaring and slapping their knees while Lizzie stood there, working her jaws in silence, wondering what they were drinking. Rufe Collins laughed so hard he fell off the chair and bumped his head on the leg of the stove, which only added to the hilarity. Poor old Lizzie left not even suspecting that she had made their day.

After the uproar died down, Rufe, rubbing his head and wiping the tears from his eyes, said, "Anyone hadn't ought to laugh, but poor old Lizzie just asks for it."

Taking a chair by the stove and lighting up my pipe, I noticed Uriah Boardman sitting there with his nose in the latest copy of *Time* magazine.

"Say, Uriah," I said, "we missed you at the funeral last week. Didn't you know we was planting Linda Bern? First time in my life I ever saw that woman with her mouth shut."

Uriah looked at me over his reading glasses and said, "I heard she died, but thought it might be another false alarm."

"What do you mean, false alarm?" I asked.

"Oh hell, didn't you know? She died once before, about twenty years ago. I've always felt sorry for her husband, Leonard. That woman made his life some miserable— nagged him nonstop day and night. Nothing was ever good enough. But Leonard just stoically went about his business and did what she asked.

"Then one night," he said. "She unexpectedly up and died. Or so they thought. She 'died' in the bed right next to Leonard. He tried, gently, to shake her away. No response. He leaned over, carefully, to see if he could feel or hear her breath. Nothing.

"As was his understated way, he got up, walked down the stairs and told the boys, 'Don't fix anything for Mother, she won't be down for breakfast.'"

"Then he went to the barn to build her a coffin.

"When he finished the coffin, Leonard and the boys carried it upstairs, rolled her into it, and carefully carried it down the winding staircase, through the kitchen, into the yard and out toward the truck. But as luck would have it, just as they got to the end of the fence, they got a little tired or grew a mite careless, and turned the corner a tad too sharp, and smacked the end of the coffin hard against the post.

"The jolt seemed to wake the dead.

"Linda sat straight up and wanted to know what in tarnation she was doin' in a coffin! She lit into Leonard and the boys something fierce. She went on to live another two decades, nagging and making them all miserable, all the time. She never let them forget the dreaded 'coffin incident.'

"Then twenty years later, Leonard woke up and found Linda had once again passed away in the bed right next to him. Once again he stoically called for the boys, went out to the barn to get the coffin, carried it upstairs, and rolled Mother into it.

"They carried the coffin down the winding stairs and into the kitchen. But this time, Leonard was a little older and got a tad tuckered. So, he stopped in the kitchen to get a cup of coffee and sit for minute. He told the boys to carry Mother to the truck and he would be right out.

"So, the boys continued on and Leonard was standing at the counter stirring his coffee when the boys walked passed the window. All of sudden his head shot straight up, he spilled his coffee, and bolted for the door all the while hollering, 'Boys, whatever you do watch out for that damn fence post!'"

"Speaking of death," I said. "Do you remember Chester Woodcock? I can't help but remember the time his wife died. It was right in the middle of haying season, so he no more than got her under the sod when he up and married young Nellie Hawkins from over to Monroe. He needed someone to care for the livestock and put up his dinner pail, you see. Of course, he would never admit that she was also young and pretty—he was all business, that one. They stayed home for the honeymoon and went to bed early, as was his custom.

"Well, some of the folks in town decided to have some fun, so a bunch of us gathered outside the house for a shivaree, to make sure Chester and Nellie didn't get much sleep. We were having a grand time, wishing them well, in a way, when, all of a sudden, out comes Chester, all haired up, and he looked all around and said, 'What the hell is the matter with you people? Don't you have any respect for the dead?!'"

🌲🌲🌲

"Hey, Kendall!" Stan Pinkham yelled from the far corner of the store. "Do you remember Harry Plummer?"

"Yes, I remember him well," I replied. "He and his brother used to raise pigs way out on the Back Cove road. One spring they began to lose pigs one at a time, and he thought it might be on account of a bear, so he sat up all one night with his rifle sticking out of the bedroom window, pointed right at the pigpen. Just before dark he had hung a lantern on the gatepost, and he figured that if it was a bear, he stood a pretty good chance of getting it.

"About three in the morning he was dozing off, but he came to just in time to see an old she-bear coming out of the pigpen with a shoat under one arm, walking on her hind feet, and holding up the lantern with the other paw. Harry said he drew a bead on that bear's forehead and was just about to squeeze the trigger when that bear turned around and blew out the light."

🌲🌲🌲

"Not only was Harry the biggest liar in this town, he was also the worst poacher, too," Ira added. "As a matter of fact, he bought two pounds of beefsteak here just a few days before he died. I asked him how come he was buying meat, and he told me that he was forced into it because the deer out his way were getting too smart.

"It was always his way to find an apple orchard where the deer tended, and early in the evening he would climb up a tree with his rifle and a flashlight. After it got dark, the deer would come out and feed. He'd turn on the light, pick out a pair of eyes, aim between them, and shoot. This went on for a few years, but according to Harry, them deer finally wised up and caught on to his strategy. The last few times he tried to hunt like that, the minute he snapped the flashlight on, every one of them deer would close one eye."

🌲🌲🌲

"Old Harry really put his foot in it the time he came out of the woods and met Cal Dyer for the first time," Rufe Collins said.

"Cal said to him, 'How's the hunting?'

"Harry said, 'Not bad at all. I killed three deer before breakfast.'

"Cal asked, 'Do you know who I am?'

"Harry replied, 'No.'

"Cal said, 'I'm the new game warden for all of Waldo County.'

"Harry asked, 'Do you know who I am?'

"Cal said, 'No.'

"Harry said, 'I'm the biggest liar in the whole State of Maine.'"

🌲🌲🌲

"Harry used to brag about that coon hound he called Virgil," Stan Pinkham said. "Claimed he didn't even have to go into the woods himself—all he had to do was take a board which he used to stretch coon pelts while they were drying, show Virgil the board, and he would take off into the woods and later bring back a coon of just the right size to fit the board, exactly. Some smart that dog was.

"Then one day his wife asked Harry to fix her ironing board, so he came out of the house carrying it, and headed for his workshop. Without thinking, he walked right by Virgil. That dog took one look at that big old ironing board and headed for the woods. No one has seen him since."

🌲🌲🌲

Ira chimed in next.

"Harry was not a man that was easily impressed. He was down on the shore one time looking for poles to fix his pigpen, and there was a fella from Rhode Island in a duck blind. A mallard made a pass over his tollers, the man shot it, and as soon as the duck hit the water, the hunter sent his dog out to get it. The funny part of it was that the dog walked out on the water, picked up the duck, and walked back again to the blind—nothing wet but the bottom of his paws. A little while later the exact same thing happened again—the hunter shot a duck and that dog walked on top of the water to retrieve it and bring it back. Harry kept talking to the hunter but he did not make any comment at all about this unusual retriever.

"The hunter couldn't believe that Harry wasn't impressed enough by a dog that could literally walk on water to say anything. Finally, he couldn't take it any longer and asked Harry, 'Don't you notice anything unusual about my dog?'

" 'Sure,' Harry said. 'Poor thing can't swim.' "

🌲🌲🌲

Meanwhile, Uriah Boardman had been sitting by the stove, still reading the paper, alternately chuckling and grumbling over the articles.

"I just don't know what this world is coming to," he said in disgust. "According to this crime report, a car is stolen in Boston every twenty-two minutes. Why, in the name of common sense, don't they take that car and hide it somewhere?"

Uriah is always unreasonable at the very mention of Boston. Hates the place. He took a trip down there a few years ago to visit his daughter, who had just moved to the city, and it was an experience that he never forgot. On the way down, he was just sitting there on the train, minding his own business, when the conductor came along and said to him, "You can't leave that suitcase in the aisle," and continued on his rounds. Later he came back through and said, "I told you, you can't leave that suitcase there—it's blocking the aisle," and went on his way again. On his next trip through Uriah's car he yelled, "I warned you not to leave that suitcase there!"

He picked it up and threw it right out the door, then looked at Uriah and said, "There! How do you like that?"

Uriah looked him right in the face and eyes and said, "I wouldn't, if it was mine."

At the time, Uriah's daughter was temporarily living on an upper floor of a tall hotel in Boston. Uriah had never seen such a big building before. He said the roof was so high up that a man wanted to commit suicide by jumping off the top, but he starved to death before he hit the sidewalk. Another man, he said, died in the night and they were so high up that they had to carry him down two flights to get him into heaven.

Anyway, one morning he went down to the lobby to buy a newspaper. They had a big rack of papers from all over the world spread across the newstand, but he couldn't find the one he wanted, so he asked the clerk for a *Belfast Journal.*

"Belfast?" The clerk said. "I don't even know where Belfast is."

"Well," Uriah said. "If I was you, I wouldn't admit it; everyone in Belfast knows where Boston is."

We always got a good laugh when Uriah recounted his experiences in the big city, but what happened to Fred Coombs was much worse. He was in Boston on business, and he no sooner got there than a blizzard struck. It was one of the worst storms in history. The whole city of Boston was closed down tight and poor Fred had neither a place to sleep or a way to get out. He trudged into the Haymarket Hotel hoping to find a room. The clerk said he was full up, but under the circumstances he would fix him a cot to sleep on until the storm died out.

Having nothing to do in the meantime, Fred went into the dining room to get something to eat while he waited for the desk clerk to call him.

When the waiter came around, he suggested that Fred try the house specialty—Boston clam chowder.

Fred simply said, "I'll have a hamburger."

The waiter said, "Don't you like clam chowder? Our is world famous."

"I like it," Fred said. "But don't want it. Bring me a hamburger."

A few minutes later the head chef came to Fred's table and seemed a little agitated. He asked, "What's wrong with my clam chowder? Don't you know that people come from all over the country to eat it?"

Fred, by this time a mite peeved himself, said, "If I can't get what I want here, I'll go somewhere else."

A few minutes later he got his hamburger.

After eating, he wandered over to the desk to see if anything had turned up in the way of a room or if he should bed on the cot.

The clerk said, "You are in luck. We had an old man living on the tenth floor, and unfortunately he just died. As soon as they get his room cleaned out, it's all yours."

Later that night, Fred was in bed just about asleep, when a lady in white came into the room. She had been caring for the previous guest and no one told her he had died. She walked right over to Fred's bed. Without even turning the lights on, and before he realized what was going on, she pulled the covers off him, rolled him over, and gave him an enema.

Well, Fred doesn't know exactly what happend, but if you should mention the Haymarket Hotel, he will warn you: "Whatever you do, don't refuse their clam chowder, 'cause you're gonna get it one way or another."

🌲🌲🌲

Meanwhile, everyone at the store was in peak form.

"Say, Ira," I asked, "how cold was it out to your place this morning?"

"Only three degrees below zero at six a.m.," Ira replied. "Must be warming up some; days are getting longer now, and yesterday, it was eight degrees below. Still cold enough to freeze two dry rags together."

"I'm glad I didn't live back in the real old days," I added. "Heard my Uncle Curt say that in those days, it was a common sight after a snowstorm to see a man poking around with a pole, trying to find his chimney. He always said the only way to get out of the house in the winter was through the attic window on snowshoes. That was back when I was a boy, and I used to wonder—with all that snow, what was the point of leaving the house at all?

🌲🌲🌲

Uncle Curt loved stories.

One time, he was telling some summer complaints that he was out picking blueberries when all of a sudden a great big bear stood right up in front of him and let out a helluva growl. Uncle Curt saw that bear and began to run as fast as he could with that bear hot on his heels. Uncle Curt kept running and running, but everytime he turned to look back, there was that bear. He just couldn't shake him and didn't know what to do. Well, they kept running that way for a while longer. Finally, Uncle Curt said, the only way he could get clear of that bear was to run across Round Pond. It had frozen just thick enough to support his weight, but the bear, being much heavier, broke through the ice, and Uncle Curt got away.

All the while the summer people were listen at rapt attention. But after Uncle Curt finished the story, one woman was a little skeptical.

"Now hold on a minute," she said. "You said were picking blueberries when the chase started—that had to be in August, right?"

"Yes, it was," Uncle Curt replied.

"Then you escaped by running across a frozen pond? Now, I know Maine is famous for its unpredictable weather, but that's pretty hard to swallow."

Uncle Curt, paused for a minute, then said, "Oh, I guess I just forgot to tell you that the bear chased me from August to Christmas!"

🌲🌲🌲

"Speaking of cold winters, my father worked in a lumber camp back in the day," Ira said. "He told me about two lumberjacks who were working side by side, limbing two fallen trees. The trees were about ten feet apart, and they were each walking along on top of the trunks, cutting off the limbs with very sharp axes. Suddenly, the head of one ax flew off, sailed through the air, and hit the other man right in the neck. Cut his head off as clean as a slice of bologna.

'Course, it was winter, and there was snow on the ground, so they just stuck his head back on and packed his neck all around with snow. Given the bitter cold weather, he had lost very little blood and he felt fine, so they went back to work.

"Come suppertime they knocked off and went into the cook shack for a feed of beans and biscuits. It was quite warm in the dining hall, and the snow began to melt while the man ate his meal. On top of that, he had put a lot of pepper on his beans, and by and by, he sneezed. His head flew off, rolled across the camp floor, fetched up against the stove leg, and killed him deader than a pump handle."

🌲🌲🌲

"No question some strange things happen in lumber camps," said Uriah. "I spent one winter working in one myself. I always thought that digging clams was the worst kind of brutal amusement, so I tried my hand at chopping down trees. One winter of that was enough to drive me back to the coast. It was just my luck to get a camp where the foreman hated everyone. They say he wouldn't hire a man if he didn't like the way he combed his hair, or if he took some other dislike to him. His name was Otis Cumberford, but we all called him Mr. Cumbersome—behind his back, of course.

"Anyway, one time this young fella came sauntering into camp just at sunup, before the day's work began, and he told Mr. Cumbersome that he wanted a job. Well, the boss didn't like the look of him; he was young, for one thing, and he wasn't very big either. I don't think he weighed more than a straw hat.

"Boss said, 'You don't look like a lumberjack to me, but take this ax and let me see you fell a tree.'

"Well, sir, that kid took that ax and dropped a tree with one cut! The boss stood there with his eyes bugged out for a minute, and when he recovered he said, 'I'm impressed, yes, sir. But I thought I knew all the top-notch men in these woods. Say, where did you work last?'

"The young fella said, 'In the Sahara Forest.'

"Boss Cumbersome asked, 'You mean Sahara Desert, don't you?'

"The kid replied, 'Well, it is now.'"

🌲🌲🌲

"I was only in that camp that one winter, and that was enough for me," Uriah continued. "Hard work from sunup to sunset. We got enough to eat, but it was mostly stuff no one liked. In fact, someone asked the owner of the operation how he could afford to feed such a large crew of men, and he said, 'That's simple: I find out what they don't like and give them plenty of it.'

"The owner's name was Eben MacTavish, an old country Scot, closer than the next minute with a dollar, and to see money wasted was the biggest aggravation he could imagine. The old goat was always raving about the cost of equipment and finding fault with the men for misusing it. It wouldn't have been quite so bad if he'd stayed in Bangor where he belonged, but he was so afraid he might miss out on something to complain about that he was always hanging around, watching the operation.

"There was a big log drive that year, and on three different occasions, men were walking the logs, keeping them clear of snags in the river, and, as will happen, they slipped and fell in. Every time this happened old Eben was right there watching, and the minute a man went into the water, he'd holler 'Save his peavey!'

"He couldn't care less about the man, but them peaveys cost two dollars and fifty cents each, and were harder to come by than a log driver.

"Anyway, this went on, until one day, old Eben—thinking to get a better view of the drive—was up on a high bluff overlooking the river, standing up in the bed of his truck. His hired driver had the thing backed up right to the edge of the bluff, but old Eben kept yelling at him to back up a little more so he could see better. Finally, after Eben swore at him to get closer, the hired driver slammed her into reverse and she lunged backwards, dropped over the edge, and the whole shooting match plunged into the river. Without batting an eye, the drive boss yelled out, 'Save his peavey!'"

🌲🌲🌲

"You remember old John Dodge from over to St. John, New Brunswick? He was a woodsman. John claimed he was fishing one time and caught a trout. After he was all done for the day, he gathered up all the fish he'd caught, except one, which had not died during the day, and when he went to reach for it, that fish stood up on its flippers and backed away from him. Being unable to catch the thing, he decided to give it up for a lost cause, and he started for the camp, walking up the tote road.

"He'd only gone about a hundred yards when he heard a strange sound behind him. Turning around, he was some surprised to see that trout following him home. And it took a lot to get a rise out of old John.

"The next day he came out of the camp and there was that fish, rolling around in the pine needles and looking like he was having a grand old time. Every time John went to the woodpile or the privy, there was the fish, following him just like a dog.

"After a while, it got to where the fish would come right into the camp, and he finally ended up sleeping on a wet rag by the woodbox. This went on all summer, 'til one day, John headed out to go fishing again. He gathered up his fishing gear and headed for the brook. Sure enough, that fish was tagging along right behind him. To get to his favorite fishing spot on the other side of the brook, John had to cross over an old footbridge. Well, John began to cross the bridge with that fish flopping along right behind him. About halfway across there was a wide crack in the boards. John stepped right over the crack, but it was too wide for that fish. He flopped right through the crack, landed fin first in the brook below, and I'll be damned but that fool fish sunk to the bottom and drowned!"

🌲🌲🌲

Picking up my can of tobacco and heading for the door, I said to them, "That's it; I've got work to do, and the day is half gone, showing no profit at all."

The old car started, after considerable effort, and I headed for home, pondering over whether or not I should have a hand choke installed, as Junior had suggested. On the whole, I still think it would be cheaper to just quit smoking.

Chapter 6

An Afternoon with Asa

I saw a robin this morning, on my way out to the wood-pile. I was just looking around, like you do in the early spring, and it flew right past my head.

About four p.m. I was sitting on the piazza, enjoying the sun and watching the snow melt, when the mailman pulled up out front and stuffed something into my mailbox. My box is the last one on his route, so he was sitting in his car, lighting his pipe and getting ready to call it a day.

"Afternoon, Asa," I said. "Got time for a glass of mulled cider?"

"No thanks, Ken," he says, "but I might have a cup of coffee if you have one kicking around."

"Sure thing," I told him. "Come up on the piazza and make yourself at home."

There are few things in life that give a man more pleasure than sitting on a piazza in the spring sunshine with a good cup of coffee and an old friend to swap a few yarns with.

Asa's mind was on a different tack, however, and he sat back in the old rocker and said, "I was just thinking about the last time I took a drink of hard stuff. It was just twenty-eight years ago this spring. In those days I was building boats and, on occasion, coffins, too. Early one morning the undertaker, Wallace Mallett, came to me and said, 'Asa, I've got to have a coffin by tomorrow night.'

"Gorry, Wallace," I said. "It's awful short notice, ain't it?

" 'Well,' he said. 'How much notice can you expect on such a job? Seriously now, I know it's a lot of work in a short time, so I brought you a jug of Old Melody to help the job along.' "

"Well," Asa continued, "I was just finishing a catboat for Joe Fisher's son, so as soon as the tiller was set in place, I went to work on that coffin. I didn't spare myself any, and I didn't spare that Old Melody, either. I worked on it all night, and it was finished just as the jug was finished, just before daylight.

"The next day, around noon, Wallace came to the door and asked if the coffin was ready. We walked out to the workshop, I opened the door, and I noticed that Wallace had a funny look on his face. I looked in, and there was that coffin, but she had a rudder and a centerboard on her!

" 'Godfrey mighty,' he said. 'Do me a favor, will you? When I kick the bucket, make sure someone else builds my coffin. I don't want to sail into the great beyond looking like I'm not taking it seriously!'"

🌲🌲🌲

Looking down the road toward town, watching the snow melt and form little rivers that merged and became fair-sized streams in the deep ditches on both sides of the road, I was thinking of the old days, when all the roads were dirt and spring was called Mud Season. After a winter of uncommonly deep snow, the roads were impassable quagmires for a couple of months.

"One particularly muddy spring," I said to Asa. "I was standing on this very spot, and suddenly, I spotted an object working its way up the road. Couldn't figure out what it was. It was about the size of a cat, but cats don't walk in the mud if they can help it, and I knew it wasn't a woodchuck—too early for them. Besides, a woodchuck would be moving along the stone wall, not in the middle of the road like that.

"About two hours later it came up even with the house, here, and I could see it was a hat. Well, I thought I recognized it, so I walked over to it, and when I got close enough I could see it was old John Prince.

"Kinda muddy walking, ain't it, John?" I asked.

"He looked right up at me and said, 'Oh hell, I ain't afoot—I'm on horseback!'"

"I don't remember that," Asa said. "But I do recall that old John was probably the most stubborn man who ever lived. I told him one time, 'John,' I said, 'you are so stubborn and contrary, if you ever fell in the river and drowned, we'd look for your body upstream.'

"In fact, he was so pigheaded, people used to make up stories about him," Asa said. "I heard one time that it came suppertime, and old John was nowhere to be found. They checked the barn, woodpile, and the privy, but he was nowhere about, so they sent his grandson, Willie, out to find him. Willie looked everywhere, and kept getting farther away from the house.

"Finally, he looked up, and there was old John, standing in a thicket out back of the woodlot. Willie told him supper was ready, and trotted back to the house. They all sat down to eat and old John still didn't show up, so Willie was sent out again to see what was keeping him.

"Willie found old John still standing in the same spot, so he asked if he was coming to supper.

"Old John said, 'Nope.'

"Willie said, 'Why not, Gramp?'

"Old John said, 'I'm standing in a bear trap.'"

"You know," said Asa, "One of the things that people from away can't seem to understand about Maine people is that we do tend to be brief in our speech. Old John was certainly a man of few words, as they say. Far as I'm concerned, I don't see any point in continuing to talk when you've said your piece. Anything I can't abide is someone who keeps talking long after he's made his point."

"Sometimes a few words is all that's necessary," I said. "Last summer I was talking to a fella from Connecticut, and he was telling me about an incident up in Lincoln. Seems he had this hunting camp out in the woods up there, and one winter there was a much heavier snowfall than usual, so he came up on a weekend to shovel off the roof so it wouldn't cave in.

"Well, he drove in as far as he could, then he started walking. Just as he crossed a brook he noticed a little boy skatin' on the ice, and while he was watching, the boy fell in and went right under the ice. Of course, he beat it right down there and grabbed the kid by the collar and pulled him out onto the bank. He asked the boy where he lived, and he said, 'Just a little way, if I cut through the woods.'

"Well, the boy went home and the fella walked in to his camp, started the fire, and poured himself a stiff drink. While he was sitting in front of the fire, thinking about what a close call that boy had had, he heard a knock on the door, and when he opened it, there was this middle-aged woman standing there.

"She asked 'Are you the man who pulled my little boy out of the brook?'

"The fella said, 'Yes, I am.'

"She said, 'You didn't happen to see what became of his mittens, did you?'"

"That sounds about right," Asa said. "I'm reminded of that family of summer people who own that big place out on Duck Cove. A few years ago they all arrived here for the summer, and that oldest daughter of theirs—Jayne, I think her name was—seems she had a boyfriend back in New York City, and she was some put out, being forced to spend all summer here without him.

"Anyway, she was walking around all huffy and feeling hateful, finally walked right up to John and said, 'Say, what do you do for excitement around here, anyway?'

"Old John just looked her in the eye and said, 'I wouldn't know, I've never been excited.'"

"I miss Old John," I said.

"I remember my father telling me about old Mrs. Prindall years ago," I said. "She and her husband owned that old mansion out on Clam Point, the one that burned down about twenty years ago. They owned a soap factory in New Jersey, and they had enough money to burn a wet elephant. Anyway, the last anyone saw of them was the time she came to the mansion right after her husband died. It was left to her to clean the place out and put it up for sale.

"The day she arrived, she put up a notice on the bulletin board in front of the old town hall that she wanted to hire a driver for the summer. Most of the men in town were either busy building lobster traps, or something, so she wound up hiring Cliff King. Well, it seems the more money some folks have, the more they like to lord it over the rustics in a place like this. On the other hand, Cliff's ancestors settled in Maine at least 150 years ago, so he wasn't the type to take any guff from outsiders.

"As I say, Cliff took the job, and Mrs. Prindall told him that his first duty would be to pick her up at the mansion— the cottage, she always called it—and drive her into town.

"Next morning, bright and early, Cliff was sitting in the wagon at the front door of the 'cottage,' and out comes Mrs. Prindall, all dolled up to impress the townsfolk. As she stepped into the wagon, Cliff remarked, 'It's a fine day for a drive, isn't it?'

"She just plopped herself down in the backseat and said, 'Mr. King, I hired you to drive my wagon, not socialize with your employer.'

"Apparently Cliff's motto was 'Don't get mad, get even,' because he never spoke another word to her all summer. At the end of the season he handed her an itemized bill for his services, and as she was reading it over, she came to an item she didn't understand, so she said to him, 'What is this item here, for five dollars?' Cliff, adopting a real haughty air, said, 'That's for sass—I don't often take it, and when I do, I charge.'

"I guess when money comes up against pride, there's bound to be an explosion. She sold the mansion and never set foot in town again."

🌲🌲🌲

"Speaking of money," Asa said, relighting his pipe. "I was in Andy's hardware store the other day, and we were discussing the economy and all. Business has been poor lately, so he was complaining about lack of trade and the value of the dollar. I told him that money couldn't buy happiness, and he says, 'Money can't buy happiness, but if you've got enough of it, you get to choose the kind of misery that suits you best.'

"I guess it has been tough for him lately. I was in there about two months ago, and Andy was gone somewhere. I asked Keith, the stock boy, where Andy was, and he said, 'He's up in town, buying more red ink.'

"I'll say one thing about that Keith, he thinks quick on his feet. One time last summer, one of them summer complaints came into Andy's place, said he wanted to buy two feet of stovepipe. Keith told him that it only came in four-foot sections. Well, this bird insisted that he only wanted two feet of pipe, so Keith says, 'I'll go out back and ask Andy about it.'

"Keith went out back where Andy was taking inventory and said to him, 'Some fool wants to buy half a stovepipe,' and just as he said it, he noticed that the fella had followed him into the back room, so Keith continued without pausing , 'and this gentleman wants to buy the other half.'"

🌲🌲🌲

A few minutes passed while Asa and I sat watching the snow melt and wondering if the coming summer would be any different from the last. After a while he asked, "How do you feel about the school board wanting to bring back corporal punishment? I hear the kids are getting pretty wild."

"It don't do any good to lick a kid," I answered. "Why, the worst licking I ever got was for telling the truth."

Asa just looked at me and remarked, "Well, you got to admit, it cured you."

Chapter 7

Getting the Car Inspected

When you live in Maine, there is a ritual which you must put up with every year, called state inspection of motor vehicles. Every time you drive into an inspection station, you just know that they are going to find something wrong and declare your car a death trap. Of course, it's never anything they can't fix for a price. I've been to other states where they have no such foolishness, and wondered why there were no more death traps on the road there than here in Maine, where they are inspected annually.

Today, it was my turn to take my car in for a checkup and to get a sticker. My car is not new, and hasn't been for some years now. As I drove into the inspection station, I knew I was in trouble when Pete Doughty, the local mechanic, yelled, "Hey, anyone killed in that wreck?"

Usually the filling station is a loose and friendly place, but at inspection time it becomes a dreadful part of an expensive ordeal. A visit to the dentist is no picnic, but a man's pocket nerve is even more sensitive. When you get between a Mainer and his wallet, you are skating on thin ice.

While Pete jacked up my car to check ball joints, the muffler, and all the other expensive parts, I went into his office to visit with the local characters who always hang around there. I knew my car would get a good going-over because Tim Hanson of the State Police was there. He was telling the boys about something that happened in court the other day, so I settled back in one of the filthy chairs to listen.

"Yes, sir," Tim went on, "you know, most people don't think of a courtroom as being very funny, but some strange things happen there. You must have heard that old Will Seavey finally got caught for poaching deer? Why, that old goat has been a poacher longer than anyone can remember—one of the all-time greats, you might say.

"Anyway, it seems he was coming out of the woods with his gun on one shoulder and a small deer on the other, but he wasn't paying much attention, and he walked right out in the face of the game warden. You fellows probably know him—a young fella from up around Portland. Everyone says he's scared to go in the woods, so he just rides around, checking licenses as the hunters are coming out of their cars. I guess he does get out of his car once in a while this time of year, checking beaver dams and so forth.

"I know he wasn't expecting to run into a poacher this time of year, so he and Will were both somewhat surprised to meet under the circumstances. The warden was just standing there by the side of the road when Will stepped out of the woods, lugging that deer and rifle.

" 'Well, what do you think you're doing?' the warden asked.

"Will said, 'Oh, nothin', just croosin'.'

"Then the warden said, 'Croosin'? What do you call that on your shoulder?'

"Old Will looked around and says, 'That's my rifle.'

"The warden said, 'No, I mean on your *other* shoulder!'

"Old Will looked the other way, jumped back, and yelled, 'Yikes! Where the hell did that come from!?!'

"Of course, even the greenest warden in the state wouldn't buy that, so he pinched Will and took the deer and Will's rifle. In fact, it was the same rifle his father used when he took after that thief, the time the old man caught him coming out of the coop with a Rhode Island Red under his arm. He yelled at him to stop or die where he stood.

"The thief stopped, looked around at the old man, and just laughed. He said, 'You're so old, you can barely stand up, let alone hit anything with that thing.'

"The old man hauled up, drew a bead, and took that hen's head off just like that." Tim snapped his fingers loudly. "That thief dropped that chicken and beat it some quick.

"Anyway, old Will wasn't too shook up about being caught, but he was real concerned about turning that rifle over to the State. Well, as I said, he made his appearance in court, pleaded guilty, and the judge fined him two hundred dollars. As he was paying his fine, in cash, this warden had to rub it in a little, so he said, 'That's pretty expensive deer meat, isn't it, Will?'

"Old Will just glanced at him sideways and kept counting. He said, 'I figure, over a period of forty years, about two cents a pound.'

"I was surprised that the judge fined him so much. Usually, these days, they either just slap them on the wrist or they jump on the arresting officer for failing to say 'May I' when he made the pinch. It's more like the old days, when I first got into law enforcement. My first case was the town drunk up in West Athens. The judge fined him thirty dollars for being drunk in public, and the old drunk says to the judge, 'Can't pay it. You can't get blood out of a turnip!'

"That judge gave him a look that would wilt a fence post and said, 'Quite so, but we can *keep* the turnip—thirty days.'"

♣ ♣ ♣

I was about to leave when Dr. Payne drove in to fill up that gas-guzzling pleasure palace he calls a car. I heard Pete tell him to turn his engine off, because the car was burning gas faster than he could pump it into the tank.

None of us could ever figure out why a man with a name like Payne decided to become a doctor. We have ribbed him about that for years, but he just grins and keeps on making huge deposits at the bank. Being a doctor of dentistry makes it even worse, but no matter how much we ride him about it, he's always been good-natured. Maybe it's because he knows that sooner or later, he will get his revenge on every one of us.

As he came into the station to pay for the gas, I said to him, as I always do, "How's the business, Doc?"

And he answered, as usual, "Oh, I just keep grinding away." If he ever thought up a new answer, we would probably wonder if he was sick.

While Pete was filling his cash register with the doctor's money, he asked, "Did you ever get them false teeth of Maynard Calderwood's to fit? He's been complaining about them for a month or more now."

Doc replied, "I've had the Devil's own works making him a set of choppers. His face is bent from the time the horse kicked him, you know. He won't admit it, so he lays it to my incompetence, even though his jaw is shaped like a fox trap a moose stepped on. But I'm doing the best I can. The first time he came in to be fitted, I sent him away knowing he'd be back, and sure enough, a week later, there he was again, saying they hurt his mouth. Well, I ground them down here and there and off he went again. A week later he was back, said they hurt the other side of his mouth this time. I worked them over again, and a few days later he was back again.

"I said to him, 'For Pete's sake, are those teeth still hurting you?' You know what the old coot said to me? He said, 'Well, I'll tell you, Doc. The old lady and me was out fishing the other day, and she hooked a big salmon. Had an awful time reeling it in, and when she got it right alongside the boat, I bent over to gaff it, slipped, fell across the gunnel, and the oar lock caught me in the groin, and for about half an hour, them teeth didn't bother me a bit.'"

🌲🌲🌲

Doc Payne has a son working for a newspaper up in Portland, and when I asked how the boy was doing, Doc grinned and started telling us about the letter he got from him a few days ago. Seems that one day things were a little slack, so the editor sent the boy out to one of the nursing homes to try and get a human interest story for the paper.

When he got there and looked around, he singled out an old man for the interview. Asked him about his life, what he had done for work and all, any vices he might have had, and finally, he asked the old man to what did he attribute his long life. The old fella told him he figured he had lived a long time because he had worked hard all his life, had never tasted any kind of alcohol, only had one woman, and his next birthday would be his eighty-seventh.

Being a typical Mainer, the old-timer had been quite brief in the telling of his story, so the boy hunted up another resident, figuring to do one more interview to make the trip worthwhile.

The second old fella told a somewhat different story. Claimed that he had only worked when he had to—and not too hard at that; he'd dug a few clams in the summer, raked a few blueberries, cut pulpwood until winter really set in, and then didn't do much of anything until spring, when the clam flats thawed out again. When asked about vices, the old fella said he drank just a little now and then, and chased just a few women—that is, up until recent years, when he forgot why he was chasing them. When he was asked why he thought he had lived so long, he said it was simply due to moderation in all things, and when asked his age, he said he was almost ninety-four.

The young reporter still wanted to be absolutely sure he had enough material for his newspaper article. He decided to do one more interview. He looked around and finally settled on this old codger all bent over in a wheelchair with a shawl around his shoulders. He had more wrinkles than last year's crab apple.

The boy asked him the same questions. The old fella told him that he had never done an honest, full day's work in his life, he had drunk enough booze to float a battleship, smoked four packs of cigarettes a day for years, chased more women than a computer could count, and otherwise, had just raised hell all his life. Stunned by all this, the boy finally asked him how old he was, and the fella said, "If I live until November fifth, I'll be forty-six."

Chapter 8

Summer Complaints

I n the summer, there are two annoying things we have to deal with in Maine: crabgrass and summer complaints. I don't know what it is with lawn mowers, but they seem to winter-kill. You leave one sitting in the shed all winter, and when you want to use it the following year, it just squats there, making spluttering sounds. Sometimes it will yank the pull-cord out of your hand as if it resents being called on to work.

I yanked and fiddled with my mower for most of an hour before giving it up. Years ago folks used to cut grass with a scythe, and the lazy ones kept goats. This fool machine probably didn't know it, but it was in danger of being replaced by a living creature. That would be a switch, wouldn't it?

It was too nice a day to be spoiled by a piece of junk, so I decided to walk to the hardware store, knowing full well that Andy wouldn't have a scythe in stock, but also knowing that the walk couldn't do me no harm. As I approached that big pine tree that marks the property line between my land and Joel Hooper's, I could see him there, and as I drew near, I could see that he was fixing the fence where a limb had fallen and broke a wire. One nice thing about walking—when you see someone you know, you stop and talk. If you are in a car you just wave and keep on going, never knowing what you missed by being in a hurry.

"Morning, Joel," I said. "You're right on the job today. That limb just fell last night; I know, 'cause it was still stuck to the tree when I went by yesterday afternoon."

"Yes," he says, "them cows of mine hang around this tree for shade when it's hot, and I don't want them to get out of the pasture and be wandering about in the road now that the summer complaints are around.

"You remember that time three years ago, my best Jersey got out, started across the road, and got run over by a summer complaint. Anyone has got to be pretty dumb to hit a cow with a car. Killed her, of course, and then he didn't want to pay for her, so I had him hauled into court. Lucky for me that old Oscar Tibbetts saw the whole thing. Oscar said that car must have been doing eighty down that road. The fella got himself a high-priced lawyer from Boston, but he couldn't shake Oscar one bit.

"He asked Oscar, 'What's your name?'

"Oscar answered, 'Oscar Tibbetts.'

"The lawyer asked, 'Where do you live?'

" 'Marshall's Landing,' replied Oscar.

" 'You lived here all your life?' the lawyer asked.

"Oscar said, 'Not yet!'

"That lawyer could see that he wasn't going to shake Oscar, so he advised his client to pay for the cow."

♠♣♠

"Reminds me of the time Old Tom, the dump tender, lost his cow," I said. "He wasn't much for mending fences, and she got out of the pasture, started across the railroad track, and a Bangor and Aroostook freight train caught her broadside and killed her deader than a doornail.

"Couple of days later this agent from the main office went to see Tom in person about a settlement. He says how sorry he was about the unfortunate accident and all, told Tom he figured the settlement should be about fifty dollars. Tom agreed, and that was that.

"About a week later, the agent was back with a voucher for Tom to sign, and Tom asks what that voucher thing was, and what it was for. The agent says Tom has to sign it to settle the claim, so Tom was about to make his mark when the agent says they had been talking it over at the main office, and they decided this accident was worth seventy-five dollars. Old Tom pushed the voucher back at the agent and allowed, 'Not by a damn sight—we agreed on fifty dollars, and I ain't payin' a cent more!'"

∗∗∗

"Yes, sir," said Joel, "this old pine tree has shaded a good many cows in its lifetime, but if the limbs keep falling off, I guess they'll just have to find another shady spot. You know, I had a herd of Holsteins years ago and about all they knew enough to do was give a lot of milk. Not half as smart as these Jerseys of mine.

"I remember one time we had a dry spell that lasted three months. Not a drop of rain, hotter than the hinges of Tophet, temperature in the nineties every day. At the time I had a cornfield right next to the pasture, and one day it was so hot that the corn got overheated, started popping. In no time, the air was full of white popcorn. Well, sir, as I say, them Holsteins were so stupid, they saw that popcorn coming down, thought it was snow, and every single one of them fool cows stood there and froze to death."

∗∗∗

Of course, I didn't let on to Joel that I didn't believe him. Someday he's apt to tell the truth, by accident, and I wouldn't want him to see any change in my reaction. I've known him for forty years now, and I'm still waiting.

After lighting my pipe and taking my time about it, I said to Joel, "You know, my great-uncle Curt told me that he had a herd of cows years ago, Holsteins they was, too. Probably during that same dry spell. According to him, it was so dry, for so long, that every cow in the country dried up except his. Claimed that just before the worst of the drought hit, he had all his cows fitted with green sunglasses, and them cows, they didn't know that the grass they were eating was all dead and brown; they kept right on giving milk as usual. One morning, some kids got into his pasture and stole every pair of them sunglasses. The next day all his cows dried up, just like everyone else's."

"Ahh, weather," I said. "My Uncle Curt used to say that if the government ever set up a weather station in his backyard, they would have to rewrite all the record books. According to him, they had a rainy spell that lasted so long, there were three babies born with webbed feet, and a man was drowned in a corncrib."

Joel's only comment was: "Would you just as soon pull that wire tight while I nail it?"

Pulling it as hard as I could, I mentioned that the post itself was loose, and Joel said, "Can't be helped. The dirt here is pretty thin; can't drive posts into bedrock. It's almost as bad as my garden. Soil is so thin, I have to plant my seeds with a shotgun."

"Speaking of gardens," I said, "Uncle Curt claimed he made a scarecrow one time that scared the crows so bad, they brought back the corn they had stolen two years back."

That seemed to get Joel's mind off fence mending, and he said, "You remember Fred Collins—used to own that farm where the Johnsons live now? He came over one time, always bragging about his garden, says to me, 'Say, Joel, I was wondering if I could borrow your crosscut saw? I've raised me some pumpkins that are so big, I'll have to cut them in half before I can put them in the wagon.'

"Now, I'll tell you, he backed off some quick when I says, 'Sure, you can have it, if you can get it. Right now it's down in my garden, pinched in a beet!'

"I'd been laying for him ever since the time my whole potato crop blighted and I tried to buy some from him. I told him I only wanted about a hundred pounds for my own use. That old goat says, 'No—I don't think I'd sell any; I just don't want to cut any of mine in half.'"

While we were finishing the fence-mending job, a grey Volvo with New Jersey plates went by, going like the hammers of Hades, and Joel remarked, "Guess we got the fence fixed just in time; the cow killers are back again.

"They can be a pain sometimes," he continued, "but some of them are fun to have around. Last summer, this tourist stopped while I was fixing this same fence, and we was just jawing about this and that. He wasn't in a hurry; in fact, he seemed quite interested in 'local lifestyles,' as he put it.

"He was looking out across the pasture there, and he says, 'Can you tell me why that cow over there has no horns?'

"So I gave him a quick lecture on cows—told him there were many reasons why cows don't have horns—Sometimes they get diseased and fall off, sometimes we have to cut them off so they don't hook each other, but, I says, the reason that particular animal doesn't have horns is because it's a horse."

"What tickles me," Joel added, "is they think *we* are the odd ones. One other time there was a fella from Texas stopped to talk to me. He didn't stay long. Asked me how much land I was working, and I told him, about two hundred acres.

"He said, 'Nice little farm you got here. Back in Texas on my ranch, it takes me all day to drive from one end of my property to the other.'

"All I said was, 'I know what you mean. I had a car like that once, myself.'"

"Look, I've got to get going," I said. "Almost forgot where I was headed."

"Come again," Joel said, and I started off to shop for that scythe.

When I arrived at the hardware store, there was quite a group of people coming and going, or just sitting on the bench out front. I got there just in time to hear Frank Rizzo trying to give Rufe Collins a hard time.

Frank had moved here from Ohio a few years back, and it has always bothered him that he has never been accepted as a native. I overheard him saying to Rufe, "For Pete's sake— how long do I have to live here before you people stop calling me 'that fella from away'?"

"Rufe replied, "Well, I'll tell you. Many years ago there was a fella who came here from New York with his parents. He was six months old when they moved here, and he grew up here—lived here all his life until he died at the age of eighty-four. We all liked him a lot, so we had something special carved on his tombstone. It said 'He was almost one of us.'

"Of course, that didn't satisfy Frank at all, so he said, 'Look, I've lived here for more than twenty years now. Three of my children were born here. Now, don't that make *them* natives?'

"No, not really," Rufe replied. "If your cat had kittens in the oven, you wouldn't call them biscuits, would you?"

Chapter 9

Rev. Tarbox

While I was milking this morning, I heard footsteps behind me, looked up, and there was Reverend Ernest Tarbox coming to the tie-up.

"Morning, Reverend," I said.

"Morning, Kendall," he replied.

I figured he was making his monthly visit to give me hell for not going to church.

"I was wondering if I could borrow your lawn mower?" he said.

"Sure, you can borrow it," I told him, "but it won't do you much good. Hasn't started since last September."

I lied a little and regretted it immediately. Always feel a little funny about lying to a preacher, but can't seem to stop. Besides, I figure they need a little something to work on, anyway. He knew I was stretching the truth, but he also knew it wasn't an out-and-out lie.

"Go ahead and take it," I said. "Maybe it will start for you."

"Reminds me of that young preacher over to Stockton," he replied. "Seems he hadn't been there very long when he heard about two brothers who had not spoken to each other for twenty years. They had a row about the ownership of a lawn mower, and never did get it settled.

"Anyway, this young preacher got wind of it and was talking to one of the brothers on the street. He said he thought it was a terrible thing that they had not spoken in twenty years, and he wanted to try and get them back on speaking terms, if he could. The preacher allowed that he had a plan, and he told the brother that he was not a betting man, but he figured he was willing to bet five dollars that the next time this man saw his brother, and if he spoke first, his brother would answer and the feud would be ended. George, his name was, thought about it for a minute, and finally agreed.

"While they were talking, George's brother appeared on the scene, coming toward them. The preacher saw him coming, so he said to George, 'Here comes your brother now. Go ahead and speak to him, and five dollars says he will answer.'

"George waited until his brother was close enough to see him and, just as his brother was about to cross the street to avoid him, he yelled, 'Hey, brother, why don't you bring back my lawn mower, you damn thief!'

"Then he turned to the preacher and said, 'You lose.'"

"Well," I said, "they say money talks."

"Yes," replied Reverend Tarbox, "but sometimes what it says is not for mixed company."

It was apparent that he was in a talking mood, so I just kept on with the milking and he started up again.

"I was just remembering my first day on the job when I came here forty-five years ago this summer. It was right in the middle of the haying season, and when I got to the church, there was only one sinner sitting there. The time came and it went. No one else showed up, so I asked that old fella if I should give my sermon anyway.

"He was a typical Downeaster—couldn't give me a direct answer—and he said to me, 'If I took a load of hay down to the pasture, and only one cow showed up, I'd feed her just the same.'

"Taking that to mean that he wanted a sermon, I went into the pulpit and preached a two-hour sermon, just as if the church had been full.

"Well, as I say, that was my first public sermon, so I was wondering if it was all right. After I finished, I asked that old-timer what he had thought of my sermon.

"He said, 'As I said earlier, If I took a load of hay down to the pasture and only one cow showed up, I'd still feed her just the same, but I wouldn't give her the whole damn load!'"

"I suppose young preachers are just like anyone else," I said. "They make a few mistakes, being new on the job and all. I'll never forget that young fella they sent to fill in for you while you were on leave. He came from the city, and really didn't know how to talk to country folks like us. He'd only been around for a week or two when he started finding fault with the church. Said it was too dark and not very classy.

"Well, he hit on an idea to not only brighten the place up but to also give it some class at the same time. What he had in mind was installing a chandelier—one of them fancy, expensive ones. He made his announcement in church about what he wanted to do, and said he was going to pass a special plate around to take up a collection just for the chandelier. The plate came around, but old Billy Carpenter, who is widely known to be tight with his money, just sat there and let it go by without giving the 'extra dollar' the preacher had asked for.

"After the sermon, the preacher was standing by the door, thanking everyone for their donations, but when Billy came by, he just stood there, looking at him. Billy knew the preacher was watching him during the collection, so he said, 'I didn't put an extra dollar in the special plate, and I've three good reasons why: One, I didn't have an 'extra dollar'—I've never had an 'extra dollar.' Two, you want to buy one of them chandelier things, and there ain't a soul in this town who knows how to play one. And three, if you want to brighten up the church, why don't you do something about the damn lights?'"

🌲🌲🌲

"While we are on preacher stories, I was wondering if you ever heard of that old-time preacher who was asked to pray for rain?" I asked the reverend.

He just stood there, looking puzzled, and admitted, "No, I don't know as I ever did."

"It seems," I began, "that down in Oxford County there was an old minister who had been at it for years, and, after a long spot of hot, dry weather, the folks in his congregation were really up against it. Cows dried up, crops failed, wells went dry, and all that. Matter of fact, they had a funeral and they had to prime the mourners.

"Anyway, this dry spell became quite a worry to those people, so, one Sunday the minister was handed a note during his sermon. After he had finished his sermon, he announced that he had been requested to pray for rain. The old fella looked out the window at the weather vane on top of the nearest barn and said, 'I'd be happy to pray for rain, but I can tell you right now, it won't do a bit of good unless that wind changes.'"

🌲🌲🌲

"Sounds like he was more practical than faithful," replied the reverend. "Reminds me of them two lobster fishermen down to Rockland. They was more faithful than practical. Seems they were out hauling their traps when a storm came out of nowhere. Raining like the heavens had opened up, wind blowing a living judgment. She started to take on water, and they pumped and bailed but it was coming in faster than they could handle it, so, finally the skipper said to his helper—who wasn't wrapped very tight, as they say—'This boat is sinking. If you know any prayers, you better say 'em.'

"The helper allowed that he didn't know any prayers, as such, but he said that he used to live next door to a Catholic church, and he could hear what they were saying, sometimes. The skipper said, 'That's more than I can offer—go to it.' With that, the helper got down on his knees in the bottom of the boat and said, 'Under B-15 . . .'"

🌲🌲🌲

The milking was done by this time, and we were walking back to the house.

"Back a few years ago, Reverend, I got lost up in Macwahoc. No road map, couldn't see any signs, so I stopped and asked this fella, who didn't have a full sea bag, either, and he had no idea how to direct me to Bangor, so I started to drive away. Hadn't any more than got under way when I heard him hollering and, looking in the mirror, I saw him and another fella, running after my car. 'Course I stopped, and he came running up alongside my car and said, 'This is my cousin; he don't know the way either.'

"After a while, I came to a gas station and got directions. The fella in the gas station told me about a tourist who got turned 'round in the same area; said this fella and his wife were driving around and all of a sudden, he was faced with three roads and no signs. He decided to stop at a little store and ask directions. Well, that storekeeper was a typical old Downeaster, mighty short on words and all. The fella left his wife in the car, went into the store, and asked, 'There is a road out here that goes off to the right; can you tell me where it goes?'

"The old storekeeper simply said: 'Macwahoc.'

"That didn't mean anything to the tourist, so he said: 'That road that goes straight—where does that go?'

"The storekeeper answered: 'Passadumkeag.'

"Still confused, the tourist said, 'Okay. If I take the left fork, where will it take me?'

"The old fella simply answered, 'Wytopitlock.'

"The tourist got back in his car. His wife asked if he'd found out where they were, and he replied, 'Good Lord, no; that fella can't speak a word of English!'"

Chapter 10

Hunting Season

Fall is probably my favorite time of the year. The weather is usually quite pleasant—warm during the day but plenty cool enough to sleep at night. Matter of fact, about the only fault I can find with fall is that winter comes next on the season schedule, and not far away at that. Each day is a little shorter than the day before until just like that it is finally winter and we don't hardly get a day at all. Winter days in Maine seem more like nights that just ain't quite as dark.

The deer-hunting season opened two days ago, so a bunch of us got together and drove up to my camp on Mopang Stream. We saw one deer on the way into the camp, and Jake Morgan made a halfhearted attempt to get out of the car and take a shot at it, but it was moving so fast, I doubt that a bullet from that old .30-30 of his could have caught it, anyway. Besides, no one wants to shoot a deer the first day of hunting season. If the weather is too warm, it's apt to spoil before you can get it home, and, if you leave it hanging outside the camp, a bear might get it some dark night.

These hunting trips are 'bout all the same: More deer are killed in the camp than in the woods. When a bunch of hunters get going on game stories, the hair and the blood gets pretty deep on the camp floor. I know for a fact that Rufe Collins hasn't killed a deer for at least ten years, but by the tales he tells, you would think he was Maine's answer to Buffalo Bill.

As usual, after supper we were all sitting around the table, playing penny-ante poker and trying to top each other. Poor old Diogenes wouldn't have hung around there very long.

There is always one in the crowd who doesn't join in on the games or the storytelling—or anything else, for that matter. I've known Sonny Kelley for years, and I've never known him to do anything but sit around and concentrate on doing nothing.

He reminds me of that old duffer they tell about who went to a summer resort and just sat around doing nothing all the time he was there. That particular year, they had a brand-new social director, and she was some busy, making sure everyone was having a good time. Well, this old duffer was there mostly because his son had talked him into going there with him, thinking it would do him good. By and by, that young social director spied the old fella just sitting on a bench all alone, doing nothing, so she rushed right over and started talking to him.

"Would you like to play tennis?" she asked.

The old fella simply said, "Nope—tried it once, didn't like it."

Not being one to give up to easy, she asked, "How about some badminton?"

The old fella said again, "Nope—tried it once, didn't like it."

Then the young lady said, "Okay, then, why don't you come with me, and we'll go swimming?"

The old fella said, "Nope—tried that once, too, didn't like that either. But that's my son over there; he might like to go swimming."

The young lady was a little put out with him by now, and replied, "He's an only child, I'll bet."

🌲🌲🌲

Stan Pinkham was dealing the cards, and telling about the first time he ever drove over Route 9, what we call "The Airline." It runs between Bangor and Calais, through one of the most desolate areas of Maine. Years ago it was narrow and crooked—wasn't even tarred for long stretches at a time.

"Never saw anything like it," Stan was saying. "Miles and miles of nothing but miles and miles. If a man ever got broke down on that road in a new car, by the time anyone else came along, they would probably tow his car direct to a museum. There was one real bad piece of road . . . I saw the sign that said 'Road under repair.' What it didn't say was that they had taken it into the shop.

"At the time I had an old Chevrolet," Stan recalled, "which I thought would go almost anywhere, but she went into a water hole clear up to her running boards and fetched up solid.

"Well, there I was, figuring out my next move, when a fella came along with a team of horses and wanted to know if I could use some help. I told him that I'd like to trade even, the car for one of the horses, but he couldn't see that; said he'd twitch me out of there for five dollars. I thought his price was a little steep, but paid him anyway. He hooked that team on and they just walked off with that car like it was an empty buggy. 'Course, I thought I'd been taken, and I wasn't too happy about it, so just as I drove away I said to him, 'You know, for five dollars a tow, you could hang around here and make a fortune, hauling cars out of there day and night.'

" 'I do a lot of towing during the day, but not at night,' he said. 'At night, I haul the water for that hole.'"

"How come none of you guys have seen any deer yet?" asked Uriah.

Grover answered, "All I've seen so far is a couple of tracks, but 'course, that only shows where they were, and I want to know where they are now."

Ira added, "I still think the deer are scarce on account of the moose; deer just won't stay around where there are moose."

That argument had been going on for years, so to keep it from starting up again, I said, "I don't know why it is, but it seems to me that there are less deer now than when I built this camp. That first year I had the best luck I ever had, before or since."

🌲🌲🌲

"Pretty good," said Ira. "The best luck I ever had was the time I went into the woods with only one bullet to my name. This was during some hard times, and everything was hard to come by, even ammunition.

"As I say," he continued, "I was walking along, wondering how I was going to get through the winter with very little money and not much food in the larder. Suddenly, right in front of me, not twenty yards away, were two beautiful silver foxes. Even in those days, a silver fox pelt was worth a pretty penny, and here I was with two of them within range, but only one bullet.

"Standing between them was a big flat rock, shaped like an old-fashioned gravestone. 'Course, I was some tempted to play it safe and shoot one of them foxes, but, instead, I aimed right at that rock and fired. The bullet hit the rock, broke it in two, and killed both foxes. The kick from the gun knocked me backwards into a brook, and when I regained my senses, my right hand was on a beaver's tail, my left hand was on a mink's head, and my pants button had popped off my fly and killed a partridge!"

About Kendall Morse

For decades, Kendall Morse has been a multitalented entertainment force. Born and raised in Machias, Maine, the grandnephew of a renowned local storyteller, Kendall began telling stories professionally in the early 1970s. He hosted a show on Maine Public Television called *In the Kitchen*, wrote a book by the same name, and released a popular album called *Seagulls and Summer People*. Kendall was also a successful folksinger. Three times he was voted Folksinger of the Year by the Maine Country Music Association. He was inducted into the Maine Country Music Hall of Fame in 1995, and was nominated for a Grammy in 2009 for his role in the double CD, *Singing through the Hard Times*, a tribute to Utah Phillips. *Father Fell Down the Well* is a wonderful collection of traditional Downeast stories collected and performed by Kendall during a career of performing in Maine and across America.